Contents

Introduction

At the start of the 20th century, there was almost no 'serious' American drama. Few, if any, American plays written before 1900 seemed destined to have any lasting value. Nevertheless, by the end of the century, the roll call of distinguished American dramatists included Eugene O'Neill, Arthur Miller, Tennessee Williams, Edward Albee and David Mamet. If the names of Elmer Rice, Clifford Odets, Lillian Hellman and Sam Shepard, among others, are added to that list, then it can be seen that the advance made by American drama in the 20th century was substantial.

'Popular' and 'serious' theatre

Perhaps an explanation is required about the term 'serious American drama'. After all, for many people American theatre means musicals or musical comedy, and it is true that American musical theatre frequently represented American society and way of life in an accessible style that communicated itself to audiences all over the world. Some American musicals, such as *Show Boat, Oklahoma, West Side Story* and *Guys and Dolls*, seem to prove that musicals need not always be 'mere entertainment'. The focus of this book, however, is on drama or 'serious' plays, and American musical theatre can only be mentioned in passing. The focus will be the plays written for performance in theatres by American dramatists who, consciously or unconsciously, hold a mirror up to American life and, in the process, represent American society in all its various strands: its myths, its ideals, its injustices and failures, its aspirations, dreams and politics. In studying these plays, an attempt will be made to place them in their historical, social and cultural contexts. This implies a belief that plays are written not only as a result of random impulses on the part of individual dramatists, or merely to meet a commercial need in the world of the theatre, but are also partly shaped by what is going on in a society at any given time. 'How much does this play reflect something of American society of its time?' will, then, be a recurring question in this book.

Creating an American drama

The plays and dramatists chosen for this book as exemplars of American drama mostly possess a recognisably American tone and style. By the beginning of the 20th century, European drama had produced from the late 16th century onwards major dramatists such as Shakespeare, Marlowe and Jonson in Britain, Molière and Racine in France, Ibsen and Strindberg in Norway and Sweden respectively, and Chekhov in Russia. However, America at the start of the 20th century was a relatively young country by comparison with most European nations. It did not have literary or theatrical traditions to compare with the leading European countries. American theatre, then, had to establish its own traditions and it had to fight to be regarded as equal to the best of its own domestic literature and to European drama.

We can only safely make the judgement that the best of American drama reflects important aspects of American society if we know something about the social, historical and cultural development of America itself. Plays such as *Waiting for Lefty* and *Awake and Sing!* by Clifford Odets, for example, are partly the product of their era, the 1930s and the Depression, just as David Mamet's play *Glengarry Glen Ross* is very much a play of the 1980s, reflecting an aspect of 'the spirit of its time'. To appreciate and interpret these plays, we need to know something about the specific historical, social and cultural context from which they emerged. However, the viewpoint of the individual dramatist is clearly important in this equation as well. This book intends to encourage you, the reader, to evaluate American plays within their historical and social context and, additionally, as the creations of individual playwrights who have their own viewpoints or personal signatures.

It cannot be denied that for most of the 20th century, American theatre was dominated by white, middle-class males. Black, Hispanic and Native Americans and members of other minorities have found it difficult to be heard in mainstream American theatre. Similarly, women playwrights have undoubtedly been neglected. Over the last thirty years or so, however, American theatre has shown signs that it has become more accessible to female dramatists and those from ethnic minorities. Yet even within this relatively 'closed shop' of the American theatre, the range of voices has been extensive. At its best, American theatre has reflected the diversity of American society. All kinds of American idioms and regional speech crop up in American drama, reminding us that this is a vast country with many currents contributing to the mainstream of American life. It is in this diversity that the American theatre and its dramatists find their unique voice.

How the book is organised

Part 1: A survey of 20th century American dramatists

Part 1 sets out to give an introduction to American drama during three main periods:
- the between-wars years when American drama matured and flourished during a period of great historical change and turmoil for the country
- the Second World War and the post-war years up to the election of Kennedy in 1960, during which period America became the richest and most powerful nation in the world

- the years between 1960 and 1990, during which profound social and political changes were taking place in American society.

Part 2: Approaching the texts
This part gives advice about how to read and interpret drama texts.

Part 3: Play extracts
Part 3 offers an anthology of extracts from key drama texts.

Part 4: Critical approaches to 20th century American drama
Part 4 gives a summary of critical opinion of 20th century American drama as well as a reminder of the various perspectives from which it is possible to view American plays.

Part 5: How to write about 20th century American drama
In this part, guidance is given about how to approach writing on 20th century American drama.

There are tasks and assignments, for individual and group work, in Parts 1, 2, 4 and 5.

At the end of the book are the following:
- Reading list and other resources: provides an extensive reading list of play texts, critical works, books that provide social, historical and cultural background, and other relevant resources.
- Glossary: lists and defines critical terms used with reference to drama. Critical terms that appear in bold type in the main text can be checked in the glossary.
- Chronology: provides a quick summary of historical/social/cultural events, key plays and dramatists.

This book is written for those beginning a study of American literature as part of an advanced course in English, or for anyone interested in American drama in the 20th century. It aims to encourage readers to explore beyond the few well-known playwrights, and to place the plays as they are read within the context of the development of American society during the 20th century.

1 | A survey of 20th century American dramatists

Part 1 gives an introduction to American drama during three main periods: the years between the two World Wars; the war and post-war years up to the election of President Kennedy in 1960; the years between 1960 and 1990.

- How far has the historical, social and cultural development of America shaped the plays of major American playwrights of the 20th century?

- What are the particular and personal viewpoints of individual playwrights?

- What makes the plays and play extracts studied in this book examples of major drama of the 20th century?

In the last decades of the 19th century American theatre had been largely given over to **melodramas** and lavish spectacle. Towards the end of the 19th century and in the first two decades of the 20th, America became a 'melting pot' of nationalities and cultures. Between 1900 and 1915, 14.5 million immigrants from southern and central Europe poured into the States. These immigrants, anxious to hold onto their national culture and language, were entertained at neighbourhood theatres in big cities such as New York and Chicago. Audiences enjoyed sentimental dramas about the 'old country', or about the problems of holding onto traditional mores and lifestyles in this new society of America. In the film *The Godfather Part II*, there is a scene set in just such a theatre, an Italian-American neighbourhood theatre in the Little Italy area of New York. The audience are watching a melodrama representing the problems of different generations of Italian-Americans adapting to the new society.

In European drama, in the latter part of the 19th century, there had emerged major playwrights such as Henrik Ibsen, August Strindberg, Anton Chekhov and Bernard Shaw, who were intent on representing life in their plays in a more realistic style. **Realism** in the theatre emerged from a desire to reject excessive theatrical artificiality. It represented everyday reality in a style that would seem familiar to the audiences that came to see these new plays. The dramatic language was meant to be close to everyday speech, the situations and settings akin to the kind of social problems and milieus familiar to contemporary audiences. Realism had an influence on the American stage in this period, but mainly in terms of elaborately realistic **sets**. Several years would pass, however, before the influence of the new realism meant that American drama could handle more mature themes and develop more sophisticated dramatic treatment.

Hardly any of the American plays produced between 1900 and 1915 are revived or read nowadays. At the time, however, there were large audiences for romantic melodramas with lavish but realistic settings (plays such as David Belasco's *Madame Butterfly* and *The Girl of the Golden West*, for example). Meanwhile, the new entertainment medium of the cinema was beginning to challenge the supremacy of the theatre. Soon, films would provide much more elaborate spectacle, lavish settings and 'reality' than the theatre could compete with, even though until the invention of the film soundtrack in 1927, movies were 'silent'.

1915–41: the first authentic voices in the American theatre

In 1915, American drama found its artistic feet with the founding of three new theatrical groups, the most influential of which were the Provincetown Players. The importance of these groups was that they produced the plays of European dramatists, including Ibsen and Chekhov, and that they nurtured American playwrights, giving them the opportunity to write without the commercial pressures of **Broadway**. 'Broadway' is a generic term generally used to denote mainstream, New York **commercial theatre**. Most Broadway plays and 'shows' (musicals, light comedies and theatrical spectacles) are produced by theatrical entrepreneurs for profit and are not **subsidised** by public funding.

The historical, social and cultural context

By 1915, Europe was in the middle of the First World War and America was debating whether it should stay neutral. Eventually, President Wilson persuaded the American Congress to declare war on Germany. America's participation in the war and the important role it played in finalising the Treaty of Versailles that shaped post-war Europe marked its emergence as a major world power.

In the 1920s, new assembly-line manufacturing methods produced American goods at cheap prices for mass consumption. The American economy was going through a boom time, yet recent immigrants and black Americans, especially in the Southern states, often lived in appalling poverty. American corporations such as Ford and General Motors distrusted trade unions and refused them recognition in the workplace. There was a general 'Red scare' hysteria, and anarchists and communists became the target of witch-hunts, which culminated in the notorious Sacco and Vanzetti case. In 1921 these two recent immigrants, alleged to be anarchists, were found guilty of murder on the flimsiest of evidence and were executed six years later.

The 1920s became known as the 'Roaring Twenties'. It was the Jazz Age, the era of the 'flapper' (young women who flouted conventions), mass spectator sports and the growth of the influence of the mass media, including tabloid newspapers and radio. Yet, there was widespread intolerance and racial violence, especially in the South. Fundamentalist Christian sects thrived in the Bible belt of the mid-West and the teaching of Darwin's theory of evolution was even banned in some states. The Prohibition of Alcohol Act (1919) had banned the sale of alcohol, which only resulted in the growth of illegal bars known as 'speakeasies' and the domination of organised crime over illegal drinking.

Then, in 1929, the bubble of prosperity burst and the Wall Street Crash brought economic chaos to America and the world. Unemployment rates zoomed upwards, numerous banks failed, the value of most company shares decreased alarmingly and many companies collapsed. For the next twelve years, until America entered the Second World War, the country was battling against this 'Depression'. The 'American Dream' of ever-increasing prosperity, the freedom to pursue personal goals allied to a close community ethos, the pursuit of happiness, love and the closeness of family ties, seemed to be just that: a dream.

In 1932 Franklin Roosevelt and a Democratic administration were elected on the promise of delivering a 'New Deal', which would get America back to work and prosperity. The government invested in a system of public works and gave loans and grants to help business get back on its feet. Initiatives such as cash relief for the poor, the creation of jobs by building houses, roads, bridges and public buildings, and the Tennessee Valley Authority (to aid farming communities across seven states) were attempts to turn the economic tide, but by 1938, there were still 11 million people unemployed.

Meanwhile in Europe, fascism had taken root in Germany and Italy: Adolf Hitler and the Nazi Party had come to power in Germany in 1933, and Mussolini's fascists had imposed a totalitarian regime in Italy.

In September 1939, the Second World War started in Europe. Two years later, after the Japanese bombed Pearl Harbor, America joined the war on the side of Britain and its allies. America was now on a war economy and its people went back to work.

Modernism and expressionism in the arts

During this period of great upheaval, most American artists (novelists, poets, dramatists, painters, musicians) viewed American society with growing disenchantment, which led to their alienation from the prevailing values of materialism and conformity. Writers such as Scott Fitzgerald, Ernest Hemingway, T. S. Eliot and Dos Passos became spokesmen for 'the lost generation', a term used to describe those who had been disoriented by their experience of the First World

War and who felt ill at ease in the midst of what they saw as the grossness and callousness of the post-war world, with its emphasis on production and the acquisition of wealth.

Modernism as a movement in the arts had had an impact in Europe from the 1880s on. Modernism grew out of this increasing alienation of artists from mainstream society with its ever-increasing regimentation, socialisation, urbanisation and consumerism. One of the essential characteristics of modernism was opposition to these materialistic and authoritarian aspects of modern society. Modernism seemed to advocate escape from the encroachments of a mass society that required its citizens to conform to a rigid work ethic. Not all modernists were on the left of the political divide, however. Some, for example, the poets Ezra Pound and T.S. Eliot, were politically conservative. American drama would produce several major figures during this period, some of whom would be dubbed 'modernists' and who would reflect in their plays the turmoil of these years. Dramatists would deal with new subject matter and themes, experiment with form and language, apply innovative theatrical techniques, break away from the straitjacket imposed by realism and create 'expressionist' drama.

Expressionism was a movement in painting at the beginning of the 20th century in which artists, rather than attempting to create a version of 'reality', created a highly personal vision of the world that included distorted images symbolising inner psychological states. Expressionism also influenced the other arts and had a particularly strong influence on German and Scandinavian theatre (playwrights such as Strindberg, Wedekind and Toller) and cinema (German directors such as Fritz Lang, Murnau and Pabst).

Eugene O'Neill (1888–1953)

Eugene O'Neill is generally regarded as the first major American dramatist. If escape from the constraints of conventional society is perceived as one of the recurring themes of modernism, then O'Neill's own early life can also be interpreted as an attempt at escape from an unhappy youth (arising out of an unstable and turmoil-ridden family background), as he tried gold prospecting in Honduras and a career as a sailor on commercial freighters. After a bout of tuberculosis, he decided to devote his life to writing for the theatre.

Indeed, O'Neill frequently used the personal to create drama that aimed for the universal. In his plays he represented what it was like to be alive in America in his time: the fragmentation of family life, the alienation of the sensitive individual in the face of an increasingly regimented and materialistic society, and the inability of human beings to sustain close relationships and live amicably in communities. O'Neill was associated with radical politics, but he was never a political activist as such. However, there is a latent radicalism and a critique of American society in his plays, even if his protagonists seem to settle for a doomed pessimism and a reluctant acceptance of the status quo.

O'Neill and expressionism

O'Neill was attracted to theatrical experimentation in the form of expressionism. In the theatre, expressionism attempted to depart from the realistic tradition by employing the whole range of possible theatrical expression: stylised settings, the use of masks, unusual lighting effects, creative costuming, choreography, music, sound effects and language that might be spoken in chorus or even be 'made up'. In *The Emperor Jones* (1920), for example, O'Neill uses fantastic visions and the syncopation of sound. In *The Hairy Ape* (1922), because he wants to represent workers transformed into zombie-like labourers, he demands highly stylised sets and has his characters move like automatons, wear masks and talk in monotones. Here is an extract from the stage directions to Scene 1 of the play:

> The treatment of this scene, or of any other scene in the play, should by no means be naturalistic. The effect sought after is a cramped space in the bowels of a ship, imprisoned by white steel ... The men themselves should resemble those pictures in which the appearance of Neanderthal Man is guessed at.

O'Neill describes the movements the men make as they shovel coal into the furnace of the ship:

> The men shovel with a rhythmic motion, swinging as on a pivot from the coal which lies in heaps on the floor behind to hurl it into the flaming mouths before them. There is a tumult of noise – the brazen clang of the furnace doors as they are flung open or slammed shut, the grating, teeth-gritting grind of steel against steel, of crunching coal.

Thus, O'Neill demands a staging of this scene that employs a kind of 'stylised realism'. This is an example of how expressionist theatre can communicate through non-verbal means. O'Neill's aim is to stress the dehumanising effect of soul-destroying work where individuality and human dignity are crushed. In *All God's Chillun* (1924), the stage walls are moved gradually inwards to suggest the hostile encroachment of society on a black man and white woman who have married. O'Neill, in representing the deep racial divisions in America of his time, does not offer optimistic solutions; but in his concern for the individual and the representation of society as oppressive, he displays a modernist sensibility.

The language of O'Neill

Realism, for O'Neill, was restricted to dealing only with the 'appearance of things', whereas what critic Jean Chothia refers to as 'real realism', what O'Neill was drawn to as a dramatist, dealt with 'the soul of a character'. The language O'Neill uses to evoke this 'soul of a character' aims at the poetic and represents a cross-section of American society through its various vernaculars and dialects. If America in the 1920s and 1930s may be seen as a 'melting-pot' of many nationalities and cultures, this multifaceted and shifting aspect of America is expressed in how O'Neill finds authentic voices for characters from many backgrounds. For example, here in an extract from *The Hairy Ape*, he uses a cacophony of voices to reflect the 'melting pot':

> VOICES   Gif me trink dere, you!
> 'Ave a wet!
> Salute!
> Gesundheit!
> Skoal!
> Drunk as a lord, God stiffen you!
> Here's how!
> Luck!
> Pass back that bottle, damn you!
> Pourin' it down his neck!
> Ho, Froggy! Where the devil have you been?
> I hit him smash in yaw, py Gott!
>
> *(Scene 1)*

There is an extract from *The Hairy Ape* on pages 59–61.

Classical influences on O'Neill

Although recent European drama, notably the plays of Strindberg with their emphasis on the bitterness of human relationships and on Freud's theories, was a great influence on O'Neill, he was also drawn to classical Greek drama with its emphasis on myth and archetypical dramatic figures. He took Aeschylus's *Oresteia* and, in his 1931 play *Mourning Becomes Electra*, adapted the characters and dramatic situation to a family in New England after the American Civil War. *Desire Under the Elms* (1924) had something of the same mythic quality, where repressed emotions and sexuality are explored almost in psychoanalytical terms. Part of the American Dream was the ideal of family life, but individuals in O'Neill's plays are usually portrayed as being in a process of flight from commitment or trapped tragically within the confines of a destructive family environment.

O'Neill's late plays

The Iceman Cometh and *Long Day's Journey into Night*, although they received their first productions outside the period under discussion here, were actually written in 1939. *The Iceman Cometh* deals with the theme of 'pipe dreams' which the customers of a New York 'flophouse' bar need in order to maintain the will to go on living. The tone is one of total disenchantment with the dreams that are peddled by 'dream merchants', including those 'selling' political ideals. Although it is set in 1912, the play's sense of hopelessness mirrored what many Americans felt during the 1930s as fascism in Europe gained ground, and also after the end of the Second World War when the annihilation of the human race through nuclear weapons of mass destruction seemed imminent.

In *Long Day's Journey into Night*, O'Neill represents the Tyrone family (based on his own family) not as the close knit family of the American Dream, but as a group of people who are bound together by a shared experience of conflict, guilt, dependencies and hatreds. O'Neill's representation of family life seemed to mirror the personal experience of many Americans of a generation later. In the 1950s, when this play was first produced, many Americans were becoming very concerned about what was happening to the institution of the family: divorce rates had started to rise and there was a widespread concern about the increase in juvenile delinquency. In this play O'Neill was clearly dealing with personal demons that still haunted him from his youth (sibling rivalries, the mental instability of both his parents, dark family 'secrets' associated with drug and alcohol abuse), but the play can be also be interpreted as having universal significance in relation to the family as an institution.

A strong feature of both these plays is the range of the language employed by the dramatist through the 'voices' of his characters: it ranges from colloquial American (Brooklyn dialect and Broadway slang, for example), through American as spoken by recent immigrants, to a heightened poetic language used by his poet-rebel characters. O'Neill was probably the first major dramatist to find a truly 'American voice' for the stage.

▶ Choose a scene or short extract from any of O'Neill's plays and analyse how 'American' O'Neill's voice is. Consider the ways O'Neill has his characters speak, the variety of ethnic backgrounds that are dramatically represented, as well as settings and narrative incident.

Elmer Rice (1892–1967)

Two plays by Elmer Rice deserve special attention: *The Adding Machine* and *Street Scene*.

The Adding Machine (1923)

The Adding Machine portrays the life and death of Mr Zero, a victim of industrialised society. Using expressionist techniques, Rice paints a picture of American life that stresses its conformity, injustice and inhumanity. The stage settings Rice describes attempt to suggest the essence of place. For example, in the last scene of the play, Rice describes Zero sitting by an adding machine with white papertape flowing endlessly from it until eventually it covers the stage. Through this expressionist image, Rice is attempting to convey how soul-destroying mechanical labour is choking the lives of contemporary Americans. Rice's dramatic language too is frequently non-realistic: characters speaking in unison, characters speaking their thoughts aloud. The characters are named Zero, One, Two etc.

▶ Read the extract from *The Adding Machine* on pages 61–63. What are the 'expressionist' features of this scene and how does the scene differ from a realistic theatrical representation? If you were directing the scene, what instructions would you give the two actors about how they should say their lines of dialogue?

Street Scene (1929)

Street Scene, by contrast, is a naturalistic play: it attempts to put 'a slice-of-life' on stage. **Naturalism** in drama aims to reproduce reality as closely as possible. It can be seen as an extreme form of realism. In naturalistic plays, everyday speech is employed as authentically as possible, so any theatrical or stylised dialogue is avoided. In terms of stage settings, every effort is used to persuade audiences that what they are looking at is 'real' and not just a stage set. One difference between realism and naturalism is that, in naturalistic drama, there is rarely a clear-cut resolution to the conflicts that have been represented on stage, whereas with realism there is almost always a dramatic resolution, a dramatic climax in which the conflicts are neatly resolved and solutions are offered. Naturalism is much less structured than realism, which favours dramatic closure. However, it should be borne in mind that most playwrights are not purely naturalistic nor purely realistic in their treatment of their themes, but are more eclectic, borrowing from more than one approach.

The setting in *Street Scene* is a New York street and a run-down 'brownstone' apartment building; the characters represent the melting-pot aspect of America: Italians, Swedes, Irish, Jews and Germans. The play represents the poverty and harshness of the lives of many ordinary Americans of the time, as well as their prejudices, aspirations and political attitudes.

Maxwell Anderson (1888–1959)

Maxwell Anderson believed that theatre was 'a religious institution devoted entirely to the exaltation of the spirit of man'. Despite the disillusionment that he and his generation felt during the 1920s in the aftermath of the First World War with its years of pointless trench warfare and the wilful waste of millions of lives, followed by the social collapse of the 1930s and the spread of fascism in Europe, he tried to represent human beings as struggling heroically to rise above tragic circumstances – even though they were usually defeated in the attempt. In many of his plays he aimed at poetic **tragedy**, employing verse as his mode of dramatic speech, very often interspersed with realistic prose.

Early plays

Anderson's first success was a play about soldiers in the First World War, *What Price Glory?* (1924) which he co-wrote with Laurence Stallings. The play represents war not as a heroic endeavour, but as a hell run by incompetent officers. The Sacco and Vanzetti case (described on page 11) provides the basis for Anderson's 1928 play, *Gods of the Lightning*, which he co-wrote with journalist Harold Hickerson. The police, the judicial authorities, the lawyers, indeed almost everyone in a position of power, are portrayed as corrupt and willing to bend evidence to send innocent men to the electric chair. With his emphasis on the importance of the individual and his anger at injustice meted out to the exploited by the exploiters, Anderson can be clearly identified as a radical playwright and modernist.

Winterset (1935)

In the 1930s, there was an attempt to revitalise poetic drama by dramatists such as Anderson and T. S. Eliot, and the British playwrights Christopher Fry and W. H. Auden. One of Anderson's major works was a verse play entitled *Winterset*, in which he used verse to produce a tragic intensity. *Winterset* was the first verse modern tragedy to be successfully performed on Broadway.

In the play Anderson returned to the theme of the Sacco and Vanzetti case, using the medium of poetic tragedy to deal theatrically with contemporary American issues. Mio is determined to prove his father's innocence after he has been executed for a crime he did not commit. In this speech, Mio describes an occasion when he visited his father in prison:

> When I was four years old
> we climbed through an iron gate, my mother and I,
> to see my father in prison. He stood in the death-cell
> and put his hands through the bars and said, My Mio,
> I have only this to leave you, that I love you,

and will love you after I die. Love me then, Mio,
when this hard thing comes on you, that you must live
a man despised for your father.

(Act 1, Scene 2)

Other plays

Other important plays written by Anderson include the historical dramas *Elizabeth the Queen* (1930) and *Mary of Scotland* (1934). His 1939 play *Key Largo* deals with the effect of the Spanish Civil War on its main protagonist, but its real theme is the need to stand up to fascism wherever it arises.

Clifford Odets (1906–63)

The Depression of the 1930s dominates the plays that made Clifford Odets one of the most famous American playwrights of the decade. Odets grew up in the Bronx area of New York, a tough, working-class district whose population endured some of the worst ravages of the Depression. He was born into a Jewish-American family with a tradition of radical politics. Odets took the sharp, wisecracking, street-wise vernacular of his family and neighbours and had his characters speak in the metaphors of street language.

Odets was initially an actor. He then became a founder member of the Group Theatre, formed in the early 1930s by like-minded actors and **directors** who wanted to stage new works that addressed the issues of the day from a left-wing perspective. The Group Theatre was heavily influenced by **The Method** approach to acting, which had evolved from the teaching of Stanislavsky. Stanislavsky was co-founder of the Moscow Arts Theatre in the late 19th century and had worked with Chekhov, the great Russian playwright (see page 10). The Method was meant 'to enable the actor to use himself more consciously as an instrument for the attainment of truth on stage'. Actors were meant to make use of their own emotional experiences to help them get 'under the skin' of their characters, understand their **motivation** and, rather than 'act' the character, 'be' him or her. The Method encouraged actors to be more naturalistic in their acting style and less 'theatrically' false.

Waiting for Lefty (1935)

Waiting for Lefty was Odets' first big success. It is a one-act play, an example of **agit-prop**, a term used to describe a drama that aims to stir up an audience to political action. The 1930s were a time of industrial unrest as American employers resisted unionisation, and workers struggled to achieve decent wages and working conditions. Odets uses a taxi union meeting during the 1934 New York taxi strike as the dramatic situation; arguments are put to the audience about whether a strike should be called or not. When the play was first produced, actors playing taxi drivers were planted in the audience and they would call out 'Strike!' to encourage the audience to agree. This dramatic ploy breaks down the illusion that it is reality that is being watched up there on the stage; the aim was involvement – the barrier between actors and audience had to be partly destroyed so that the members of the audience could feel personally involved and perhaps moved to direct action in their own lives. In some ways, agit-prop employs an expressionist approach, breaking through the limitations of realism in its attempt to unsettle audiences and move them to action.

Awake and Sing! (1935)

Awake and Sing! confirmed the emotional power and dramatic vitality of Odets' writing. The dramatic situation in the play is heavily influenced by the impact of the Depression on ordinary Americans, this time a Jewish family living in New York. Each member of the Berger family struggles to make a living. The play is full of emotion, rhetoric, humour and insight. The prevailing idiom is big city, New York Jewish, a mixture of street slang, ethnic words, hard-boiled wisecracks, earthy humour. There is less of a straight political agenda in *Awake and Sing!* than there had been in *Waiting for Lefty*, but Odets' sympathies are clearly still with the poor and the down-trodden.

Golden Boy (1937)

Golden Boy again has a close-knit New York family at its heart, this time of Italian origins. Joe Bonaparte has to choose between a career as a boxer or a violinist, the former being represented as a cynical way of earning quick money and the latter standing for a vocation that would lend his life dignity. The world of boxing becomes a metaphor for America in the 1930s, where the exploiters, in the view of Odets, take advantage of the need of the poor to make a decent living. The dramatic speech that Odets has his characters speak is again a mixture of slang, immigrant speech and heightened metaphor:

> TOKIO That boy stands a chance to make the best lightweight since Benny Simon.
> ROXY   On your nose!
> TOKIO He's got one of the best defences I ever seen. And speedy as the wind.
> MOODY But he won't fight.
> ROXY   A momma doll gives out better!
> TOKIO He's a peculiar duck – I want him thinking he's the best thing in shoe leather.
>
> *(Act 1, Scene 3)*

Other plays

Other important plays by Odets from this period include *Rocket to the Moon* (1939) and *Clash by Night* (1941). He had two post-war successes with *The Big Knife* (1949), which deals with the destructive effect of success in Hollywood, and *The Country Girl* (1950). Odets' best plays have an emotional force and theatrical energy, and perhaps no other American playwright wrote more tellingly about America in the 1930s.

▶ Read the extract from *Waiting for Lefty* on pages 67–70. How do you think the speeches Odets has written for Agate are intended to affect an audience? What are your own reactions to what the character says? Should dramatists 'propagandise' in this direct manner?

Thornton Wilder (1897–1975)

In terms of theatrical style and forms, Thornton Wilder may be thought of as a modernist, but his themes and 'philosophy' are certainly not anarchic, revolutionary or even overtly critical of society. Indeed, in his two major plays, *Our Town* and *The Skin of Our Teeth* (1942), he seems to stress the need for community, his love of his native land, his belief in humanistic values – as well as a general view of life as a gift from God that we often do not value sufficiently while we are alive. This does not mean that his plays do not reflect some of the injustices of his time. He does not, however, take an overtly political stance in his drama, as did some of his contemporaries.

Our Town (1938)

Our Town deliberately breaks through the illusion of reality that most plays try to create. A **Stage Manager** constantly addresses the audience in the theatre directly as an audience, reminding them that what they are seeing is not reality itself but an enactment of reality by actors, as in this extract from the opening of the play:

> STAGE MANAGER This play is called Our Town. It was written by Thornton
> Wilder; produced and directed by A ... .
> In it you will see Miss C ...; Miss D ...; Miss E ... .

By having the Stage Manager mention the name of the play, the author and the names of the actors, Wilder is deliberately breaking the illusion that what the audience are about to see enacted on stage is reality. However, whereas Clifford Odets in *Waiting for Lefty* uses this device to appeal directly to the audience for political reasons, Wilder's purpose is to remind us of the representative function of the characters and events depicted on the stage. His characters and the events his play depicts are intended to be universal in their significance.

There is practically no scenery required for the play, a deliberate decision by Wilder to allow the audience to concentrate on the universality of the place and characters. The American small-town setting of the play is meant to be perceived as archetypal, not only representative of all American small towns, but also of all communities round the world.

The characters are archetypes as well and we follow their fates down through the years (the play starts on 1 May, 1901 and ends in 1913, but there are also references to what will happen to certain characters in the future). Although great off-stage events are alluded to, it is the small events of life – the celebrations such as births and weddings, and the personal tragedies – that Wilder concentrates on to build up a picture of continuity in this tight-knit community.

Wilder's intention was to reach as many people as possible through his play. The tone is folksy and homespun. The danger of folksiness is that it becomes self-congratulatory and dismissive of anything or anyone different from the folksy ideal of community and family. However, there is enough darkness mixed in with the sunny elements of small-town America for *Our Town* to avoid the charge of being a complacent and rather smug picture of American life.

The Skin of Our Teeth (1942)

The *Skin of Our Teeth* is, like *Our Town*, a non-realistic, non-representational play about one archetypal family surviving three major disasters, the Ice Age, the Flood and War. Wilder uses a New Jersey suburban home and the boardwalk in Atlantic City, a resort near New York, as the settings where the family – who are clearly meant to be present-day Americans – just manage to survive these tribulations 'by the skin of their teeth'. He mixes the contemporary with the ancient; he has characters named after such mythical and historical figures as Moses and Homer interact with the family, and he has humorous elements such as the household pets being dinosaurs and mammoths. Again, the audience in the theatre are constantly to be reminded that they are watching a theatrical artifice, an example of modernist drama that, as in *Our Town*, portrays the spirit of humanity in a positive and affectionate light. Wilder's 'message' is gentler and much more affirmative of mainstream American life than that of either O'Neill or Odets, for example.

Lillian Hellman (1905–84)

The rise of fascism in Europe in the 1930s and the implied fear of native American fascism permeates the three major plays that Lillian Hellman wrote during this period: *The Children's Hour* (1934), *The Little Foxes* (1939) and *Watch on the Rhine* (1941). Hellman was not, like O'Neill, Odets and Wilder, an experimentalist in dramatic form; indeed, she looked back to Ibsen and the 'well-made' play. Her plays are usually classed as melodramas that deal with important social issues, pitting good against evil, moral values against amorality and selfishness, the weak against the predatory and the strong. Her villains are usually associated with money values and ruling élites; the characters she clearly approves of have social consciences and are active in fighting tyranny. Although Hellman's plays may be set in New England, New York or the American South, they aim to have universal significance.

Hellman is the only female playwright represented in this section and one of the very few women dramatists to have a successful career in the American theatre in this era. Whether her gender is relevant to how we interpret her plays is a matter of personal judgement.

The Children's Hour (1934)

Her first successful play, *The Children's Hour*, deals with the evil that slander can bring about in people's lives. Two female schoolteachers are defamed by a disturbed pupil and the resulting scandal ruins their lives, leading to the suicide of one of them. Although the play was first produced in the mid 1930s, it acquired an extra significance when Hellman was herself defamed in the 1950s and accused of being 'Un-American' by the House Un-American Activities Committee (see page 28). *The Children's Hour*, however, can be seen above all as a play of its time: in the 1930s many Americans who shared Hellman's political views felt themselves under attack.

The Little Foxes (1939)

The Little Foxes is set in a small Southern town in 1900, but its themes are clearly meant to have relevance to America in the 1930s. The Hubbard family, two brothers and one sister, stand for rapacious capitalism. They are the 'foxes' of the title, who want to prosper by any means – exploitation, racism, theft, blackmail, even murder. Indeed, certain elements of Hellman's play belong to old-fashioned melodrama – for example, in the climactic moment when Regina, the main female character, deliberately denies her husband his lifesaving pills when he has a heart attack. One of the interesting aspects of the play is how the exploitation of the black characters is represented. Hellman was well aware that the economy of the old and the 'new' post-Civil War South depended on the exploitation of black labour by white landowners and industrialists. Yet, the play can be interpreted in more universal terms as well: the Hubbards stand for fascism which has to be fought against by right-thinking individuals.

▶ Read the extract from *The Little Foxes* on pages 70–72. What do you learn about the social structure and history of the American South from this extract? Analyse the tensions between the characters.

Watch on the Rhine (1941)

Watch on the Rhine deals directly with the danger of fascism: its hero is an anti-Nazi activist who has to defend himself from betrayal by killing a fascist aristocrat. The play raises the question of what action is legitimate to defend the world against the fascist threat – and Hellman seems to come down on the side of action. It should be remembered that before the Japanese attack on Pearl Harbor in December 1941, America had been largely isolationist in its attitude to the Second World War; Hellman's play makes an earnest plea for active intervention.

William Saroyan (1908–81)

Saroyan's reputation rests mainly on his many short stories and one play, *The Time of Your Life* (1939), an almost plotless, rambling drama that, nevertheless, reflects much of what was happening in America and the world during the 1930s. Saroyan describes the play's setting like this: 'Nick's is an American place – a San Francisco waterfront honky-tonk'. The characters we meet in this bar are a microcosm of America: there are blacks, Arabs, Poles, Greeks, Irish, Italians – and a cross-section of social classes. Although the prevailing tone is comic, social injustice is more than once alluded to (poverty, police brutality against strikers, intolerance). Over the horizon is the next war. Native fascism is represented by a cop called Blick, who is eventually killed off-stage by Kit Carson, a comic braggart, resembling in some ways the mythical cowboy hero of that name. Each character has his aspirations, whether it be success in love, show business or work. Saroyan concocts a rich mixture of stand-up comic routines, dance and music. He has been criticised for sentimentality, but many perceive his sentiment as a representation of humanist values in a world intent on the quick buck and authoritarianism. However, there is no doubt about the 'Americanism' of the play. At the same time, with its premonitions of impending world conflict and its concern about the increasing conformity of modern society, it reaches beyond America and acquires universal significance.

Other dramatists and plays

Ben Hecht (1894–1964) and Charles MacArthur (1895–1956) combined their writing talents to create one of the enduring classics of the American theatre, *The Front Page* (1928), a 'screwball' comedy about newspaper life, mass hysteria, radical politics and the crassness of American society and values in the 1920s. 'Screwball comedy' is a term used to describe fast-paced comedy with lots of very bizarre dramatic incident, highly eccentric characters and wisecracking dialogue.

▶ Read the extract from *The Front Page* on pages 63–65. Show how the authors represent the cynicism of the tabloid newspaper world through the words and actions of Walter.

George S. Kaufman (1889–1961) and Moss Hart (1904–61) were another writing team to produce successful comedies that commented on American life: *You Can't Take It with You* (1937) celebrated eccentricity, individualism and non-materialistic values, against the trend of American society at the time, as does *The Man Who Came to Dinner* (1940).

Robert Sherwood (1896–1955) wrote one of the most successful plays of the 1930s, *The Petrified Forest* (1935). Its theme deals obliquely with the threat to civilisation represented by violent barbarians and, therefore, it is implied, by fascism. Another notable play by Sherwood is *Abe Lincoln in Illinois* (1939).

Marc Connelly (1890–1980) wrote *The Green Pastures* for an all-black cast, a very unusual event in the American theatre of this period. A fable based on Roark Bradford's *Ol' Man Adam an' His Chillun*, the play is about the search for God and can be fairly described as a religious parable. Its representation of black Americans as God-fearing and passive citizens probably explained why such a play came to be produced at this time, and why it found a white audience.

Assignments

1   Choose a section or scene from any play written by one of the following dramatists: Eugene O'Neill, Elmer Rice, Clifford Odets, Lillian Hellman. You may choose to use one of the play extracts in Part 3 of this book. Discuss what you think the dramatist has tried to communicate in the scene through the speech and actions he or she has created for the characters. Having identified the themes or social concerns that seem to be represented in the scene, discuss how they reflect the social and historical circumstances in which the play was written.

   Then, as individuals, write a piece on the section of the play you have discussed and give your assessment of how it represents dramatically the America of its time.

2   Choose one play written by any of the following dramatists: Eugene O'Neill, Maxwell Anderson, Clifford Odets, Thornton Wilder, Ben Hecht and Charles MacArthur, Lillian Hellman. As a group, discuss what you consider to be the meaning of the play and the relevance it has to the

period of American social history in which it was written. Discuss what viewpoint the dramatist seems to be presenting in the drama and use illustrations and quotations from the text to back up your analysis.

Then, as individuals, write an analysis of the themes of the play you have chosen, placing it in its social and historical context.

3   As a group, choose a scene from a play written during the years 1915 to 1941 that you have found both interesting and revealing about the America of this period. (You may choose one of the play extracts in Part 3 of this book.) Discuss the scene in detail in terms of its dramatic qualities, thematic concerns, and portrayal of character through language and action. Then perform the scene in any acting space (a classroom, a hall, a stage), appointing one of the group as the director and casting the roles from among the group.

Afterwards, as individuals, write an account based on your experience of the performance. Say what the exercise revealed to you about the meaning the scene had, and how that meaning could be communicated to an audience.

4   Many American writers and playwrights felt a sense of alienation from the way American society developed in the 1920s and 1930s. Referring to a minimum of two plays written during the period 1915–41, analyse (a) how the dramatist(s) represent these developments in American society in their plays, and (b) how their viewpoint becomes evident in the language, theatrical expression and action of their plays.

5   Use the glossary between pages 121 and 123, and the index to the book, to aid your understanding of the term 'modernism'. In what ways may some plays be termed 'modernist'? Refer to one or more of the extracts in Part 3 of this book to illustrate aspects of modernism as far as it relates to drama.

6   Choose what you consider one 'key' play written by (a) Clifford Odets and (b) Thornton Wilder. Compare the two plays and say how the views of American society represented by the two playwrights differ.
If you prefer, choose one play by Lillian Hellman and one by William Saroyan and write on the same subject.

7   In the 1930s, American drama was characterised by its highly political and socially committed tone. Choose one or two plays from this decade and analyse how these political concerns and views are represented in the play and how relevant they appear to the America of the 1930s.

8   Choose one American playwright who was writing during the years 1915–41 and write an extended study of his or her plays, viewing them against their social, historical and cultural background. Use close references to play text and quotations where appropriate to illustrate the analytical points you make.

9   Consider how gender or race issues surface in American plays of this period. How are women represented by male writers? How are black Americans represented by white American dramatists? Is there a discernible difference between how a female dramatist such as Lillian Hellman represents women in her plays and how male dramatists of the time represent them? Refer to a minimum of three plays in your study of this question.

1941–60: drama of turmoil and uncertainty

The historical, social and cultural context

America emerged from the Second World War as the richest and most powerful nation in the world. The economic problems of the Depression had largely been solved by the war economy and, over the next fifteen years, many – but by no means all – American citizens would enjoy a substantial rise in their living standards. However, along with victory and this new affluence, came several legacies from the war:

- Weapons of mass destruction had been used for the first time when America dropped nuclear bombs on two Japanese cities in 1945.
- The Cold War with the Communist Eastern bloc countries began. A Third World War seemed possible against the other 'superpower', the Soviet Union.
- The Cold War brought widespread paranoia about internal 'Red' subversion. The House Un-American Activities Committee started investigating Communist infiltration into American life, and writers came under particularly close scrutiny.

To many Americans in the post-war years, it seemed that the ideals and policies of Roosevelt's New Deal were under attack from an extreme right-wing conservatism. To add to the general paranoia about the Cold War and internal 'Red' subversion that characterised American society in the decade after the end of the war, the Soviet Union also developed weapons of mass destruction. This gave rise to charges that spies had delivered America's atomic weapons' secrets to the communist block and led to several spy trials, including those of the Rosenbergs and Alger Hiss. In 1948, China was taken over by the Communists. Soon after, Communist North Korea invaded South Korea, and America found itself fully committed to fighting the Korean War (1950–53). Between 1950 and 1954 the influence of the right-wing Republican Senator, Joseph McCarthy, led to widely publicised, but unsubstantiated, accusations of pro-communism and Un-Americanism against leading figures in American society.

Post-war America also had to face up to the problems of racial discrimination and inequalities within American society. The 1950s saw a renewal of the struggle for equality and justice for black Americans under the banner of the civil rights movement. Increasingly, too, American women were feeling constrained by restrictive gender roles and were campaigning not only for equal rights under the law, but also equality of opportunity in the workplace.

Many would claim that American literature and drama had come to full maturity in the 1920s and 1930s, but American writers in the two decades that followed continued to struggle to create authentically American works. The creation of the 'great American novel' or the dramatic masterpieces that would rival the best work of the greatest European playwrights such as Chekhov, Ibsen or Shaw was still the goal of most serious American artists.

It was an era when many American intellectuals and artists felt uneasy in a society that seemed to be becoming more and more of a 'mass society' (mass consumerism, mass entertainment and mass conformity). The place of the artist in such a society became an issue – and also whether it was his or her duty to register dissent about the way American society was fast developing.

Many writers became the target of McCarthyite investigation for 'Un-Americanism', subject to charges of a lack of loyalty and patriotism. This increased their alienation from a society that for them had become rampantly materialistic and increasingly philistine, as mass culture became dominated by the popular music industry, Hollywood movies, mass circulation newspapers and magazines, television and advertising. Some artists sought to protect themselves from official investigation by trying to conform to a concept of 'Americanism' and patriotism by confessing to past left-wing sympathies and by 'naming names' to investigators of friends and colleagues who had had 'communist' leanings. It was, then, a period of distinct unease during which the artistic and intellectual community were divided among themselves and distrustful of what this general pressure to conform to a notion of 'Americanism' would ultimately lead to.

It was in this era of great American power and wealth, but also widespread fear, paranoia and the rumblings of rebellion, that Arthur Miller and Tennessee Williams would establish themselves as the leading dramatists of their time. Through their plays, both would respond – albeit in very different ways – to the confusions and turmoil of post-war American society.

Arthur Miller (1915 –)

Arthur Miller was born in New York to Jewish immigrant parents. In the Depression years of the 1930s, he aligned himself with radical politics because he felt the economic system was failing millions of ordinary citizens. His origins and his experience of the Depression were very important influences in shaping his writing. In some ways, Miller resembles Clifford Odets: both are identified as radical, left-wing dramatists, although Odets was much more politically active than Miller.

Miller's early success was in a **genre** of play classed as **social drama**. In this genre, some aspect of contemporary society, an 'issue' or 'social problem', is represented on stage. This exposure of some corruption in the social fabric confronts the characters with moral dilemmas, which provide the basis for the dramatic conflict. A tightly structured plot leads to a climax in which the conflict is shown to be essentially between the ambitions and desires of the individual and the need to have society act in a just and caring manner towards all of its members.

In Europe at the end of the 19th century, the most important exponent of the 'social issue' play had been Henrik Ibsen, a Norwegian playwright. Ibsen's plays included *A Doll's House*, which dealt with the oppression of women, and *An Enemy of the People*, which dealt with civic and political corruption. Arthur Miller has often been likened to Ibsen, especially in the plays produced early in his career. Indeed, in his first successful play, *All My Sons*, he used realism in a similar style to Ibsen – an attempt to represent on the stage the social issues of everyday life, using language that approximates to everyday speech and against settings that reproduce the 'real' settings in which these 'people' would have lived. In his later plays, such as *Death of a Salesman*, he would mix realistic setting and speech with expressionist techniques, using various theatrical devices to move away from a style of strict realism.

All My Sons (1947)

Miller has stated that 'the structure of a play is always the story of how the birds came home to roost'. This is very relevant to *All My Sons*, which explores the theme of how choices made by individuals in the past give rise to consequences in the future. In the play, Joe Keller, a manufacturer of aeroplane parts, has, during the

Second World War, knowingly supplied defective engines to the United States Army in order to save his business and for what he says is the long-term welfare of his family. One notable aspect of Miller's social drama is his use of retrospective exposition. **Exposition** is how a dramatist, through language, informs the theatre audience about the characters and their dramatic situation. Exposition helps an audience understand the background to the drama and the motivations of the characters. If the exposition is retrospective, then the dramatist informs the audience of what has happened to the characters in the past and this is brought into the dramatic present, which forces the characters to face up to the moral consequences of their past actions. If the exposition is skilfully handled by the dramatist, it seems to emerge seamlessly from the present dramatic situation, while throwing light on what has happened in the imagined past.

Below is part of a speech by Joe Keller from *All My Sons* describing an important event from his past. He had been found not guilty of supplying faulty aeroplane parts to the Army and had returned home:

> Everybody knew I was getting out that day; the porches were loaded. Picture it now; none of them believed I was innocent. The story was, I pulled a fast one getting myself exonerated. So I get out of my car and I walk down the street. But very slow. And with a smile. The beast! I was the beast; the guy who sold cracked cylinder heads to the Army Air Force.

> *(Act 1)*

This speech has two main dramatic functions: it supplies the audience with important information about past events that are still resonating in the present, and it tells us the character's attitude to these events.

All My Sons reflects the guilt and denial of guilt that the war threw up, particularly guilt about the Holocaust and other war crimes, and possibly the horror many people felt at the use of atomic bombs by America against Hiroshima and Nagasaki. In the resolution of the play, Keller has to face up to his responsibility for what he has done (Miller's 'chickens coming home to roost') and kills himself – an example of how realistic plays tend to have definite closures and a rounding-off of the issues that have been raised.

Death of a Salesman (1949)

Miller's most famous play develops his recurring theme of the past impinging on the present and how it affects the members of a particular family. Willy Loman is the salesman of the title, who lives the life of a salesman with his whole being. As one of the characters says, 'He's the man way out there in the blue riding on a smile and a shoeshine'. Willy's dreams are based on the acquisition of wealth. He is what some observers at this time were calling an 'organisation man', an employee whose life was more or less totally devoted to the company he worked for.

Miller's stage directions for the play describe an expressionist set – a 'shell-like' and transparent Loman family home with no walls. When the action is set in the present, the characters behave as though they are in rooms with walls; when the action is set in the past, they walk through the empty space into another space on the stage. Whereas *All My Sons* had been essentially realist in its structure and language, *Salesman* uses an 'everyday' setting transformed by such theatrical means as sets, lighting, sound effects, music, **props** and the use of stage space to evoke past and present time. For example, here are some stage directions from Act 1 of the play:

> Uncle Ben, carrying a valise and an umbrella, enters the forestage from around the right corner of the house … He enters exactly as Willy speaks. Ben's music is heard. Ben looks around at everything.

In this play, Miller seems to be handling ideas connected with the 'American Dream': the freedom of the individual, the pursuit of happiness, wealth, popularity, personal achievement and the sense of being part of a close community. However, in a society that seems only to value people for what they can deliver in terms of profit, Willie's dreams are shown to be self-deluding. Many American writers of this era were concerned at the increasing emphasis on materialism and consumerism at the expense of developing a just and more equal society. Willy's wife, Linda, says of him: 'He's not the finest character that ever lived. But he's a human being and a terrible thing is happening to him. So attention must be paid'. Miller's humanist values shine through the thematic content. *Salesman* has been called 'a tragedy of the little man'.

A feminist view of the play, however, might well be that it is a very male-dominated world that Miller represents with the concerns of Linda, the wife, portrayed only in relation to Willy and the sons, but otherwise sidelined. However, that may be imposing a contemporary reading on a play that was written in the 1940s when the issue of feminism would have been less to the fore than it is nowadays. Very few people in 1949 would have questioned how the wife's concerns were represented in the play. Fifty years and more later, the play can be seen in the light of half a century of feminist advance and the dramatic function of the wife figure re-evaluated. The issue of whether American drama has consistently failed to represent women and their experience of American life adequately is open to debate. (See the assignments at the end of the previous section and the assignments at the end of the book.)

▶ Read the extract from *Death of a Salesman* on pages 78–80. Analyse how Arthur Miller represents the relationship between Willy and Howard through the words he gives his characters to speak. Show how the dialogue reveals who holds the power in their relationship, who is the more desperate, emotional or cold, and what different feelings the dramatist has his characters reveal through the language.

▶ Analyse the character of Linda, Willy's wife in *Death of a Salesman*, and the dramatic function she performs in the play. Do you think her concerns as a character are subservient to Willy's? How would a more feminist approach to the character and themes increase the importance of her role?

The Crucible (1953)

The Crucible is based on historical events that occurred in Salem, Massachusetts, in 1692, when accusations of witchcraft in the community led to the persecution, and execution, of men and women suspected of consorting with the devil. In his introduction to his *Collected Plays* (1957), Miller explicitly links his play about the Salem witchcraft trials with the McCarthyite inquisition in the 1940s and 1950s of those suspected of 'Un-Americanism' and communist sympathies: 'a surreal spiritual transaction that connected Washington with Salem'. (See page 28 for more about McCarthyism.) In *The Crucible*, Miller represents his main character, John Proctor, as finding the courage to stand up to the hysteria and superstition in society. Proctor goes to his death defying the investigators who want him to admit to a lie about consorting with the devil.

Miller himself became the target of McCarthyite investigation in the 1950s. In 1954, he was even denied an American passport to attend the Brussels premiere of *The Crucible*. In 1957 he was held in contempt of Congress when he refused to give names of people he knew who were, or had been, Communists. Thus, Miller, America's leading playwright, married to the most famous film star of the day, Marilyn Monroe, was thought of as 'Un-American' and potentially a traitor. *The Crucible,* in its representation of 17th century hysteria, prejudice and conformity, is a theatrical allegory of what many people considered was happening in America in the 1950s. The play illustrates how the direct personal experience of a writer involved in the social and political events of his time may be employed to produce historically significant drama.

▶ Read the extract from *The Crucible* on pages 81–83. Show how Miller suggests a rising wave of hysteria through Hale's interrogation methods, Tituba's replies and the interventions of other characters. If you were directing a performance of this scene, what instructions would you give the actors to help express this growing tension?

A View from the Bridge (1955)

A View from the Bridge is set in Brooklyn, New York. It also concerns itself with the theme of private desires coming into conflict with the moral demands of the community. Once more, the dramatic context is the family. Eddie Carbone, because of his unacknowledged desire for his niece, is drawn into betraying one of the ethical rules of the immediate community he lives in: 'snitching' to the immigration authorities about two illegal immigrants whom he has said he will help. The irony is that Eddie is behaving in a way that would be encouraged by the law of the land (informing on illegal immigrants), but for doing so, he is ostracised by his immediate family and community.

Tennessee Williams (1911–83)

Born in Mississippi, Tennessee Williams and his plays have always been associated with the American South. In the wake of the defeat of the Confederate States in the American Civil War (1861–65), an enduring mythology had formed round the idea of the 'old South' in its pre-Civil War era: of a graceful, civilised society superior to the vulgar, materialistic Northern states. Those with a vested interest in maintaining this old South' mythology clung to a belief in rural, conservative values as a contrast to what they argued was the mechanisation and vulgarity of the North. However, the myth of the gracious, civilised Southern way of life had been established on the basis of the enslavement of millions of black Americans as a source of unpaid labour. The legends of the 'old South' play an important part in many of Williams' plays.

The Glass Menagerie (1945)

This was the play that first established Williams as a major innovating force in American drama. Williams, though not attempting to write verse drama (as Anderson had done in the 1930s), still brought a fresh poetic dimension to the American stage, not only by his use of metaphorical, symbolic and heightened language, but also through his use of stage setting, props and objects, lighting, music and costume. Williams has called *The Glass Menagerie* a memory play which justifies 'atmospheric touches and subtleties of direction'. He rejects 'the straight realistic Frigidaire and authentic ice-cubes' of realistic stage settings because reality is 'an organic thing which the poetic imagination can represent or suggest, in essence, only through transformation, through changing into other forms than those that merely present in appearance' (from the introductory preface to the printed text of the play).

Williams' desperate characters try to transform reality through their imaginations, but a cruel world inevitably triumphs over this strategy for survival.

The illusions they use to protect themselves are destroyed. Laura and Amanda Wingfield in *The Glass Menagerie* are examples of these wounded, vulnerable characters that Williams created. Laura is a delicate young woman who treasures her collection of glass animals, which symbolises her own fragility and her refusal to venture out into the 'real' world. Amanda, the mother, lives in the past, essentially her youth in the South. Williams represents Amanda's romanticisation of her past as being very similar to the romanticisation of the 'old South' with its supposed civilised values, despite the barbarous reality of its slave-driven economic system. The decline in Amanda's fortunes is a metaphor for the decay of the 'grand old South' and its mythology.

Just as the Depression haunts Miller's *Death of a Salesman*, so in *The Glass Menagerie* the Wingfields are represented as suffering from the effects of harsh economic circumstances. The gap between the mother's pretensions and the genteel poverty the family lives in is shown to be wide. The disenchantment that characterises the tone of the play partly stems from the retrospective exposition by Tom Wingfield, the son of the family and presumably the dramatic surrogate for the dramatist himself, on events in 1938, when the main action of the play takes place, from the perspective of the immediate aftermath of the war. (See the use of exposition in Miller's plays, pages 29–30.) His sense of loss and alienation from society could be said to represent the feelings of many Americans in the immediate post-war period: unease about the legacy the war had left and a profound insecurity about what the future would hold for them.

A Streetcar Named Desire (1947)

A Streetcar Named Desire is set in New Orleans in the American South in the immediate post-war period. The working class male characters have served in the American armed forces and are trying to make a life for themselves after the upheavals caused by wartime absence from home.

Blanche Dubois, a fading 'Southern belle', lives her life with the protection of her illusions and depends on 'the kindness of strangers'. Blanche comes seeking refuge with her sister, Stella, who is married to the macho Stanley. She criticises Stella for having done nothing to save the family plantation, Belle Reve. In translation, the name means 'Beautiful Dream' and symbolises not only Blanche's lost innocence and faded gentility, but also the decay of the mythical South.

Stanley Kowalski, Stella's uncouth husband, can be seen as representing the flesh in the play, while Blanche stands for the soul. In their numerous confrontations, she goads him by calling him an 'ape'. Stanley finds out about her past, which includes a marriage at a young age to a man who subsequently committed suicide. In the end, he rapes Blanche, which results in her seeking a final refuge: an almost total detachment from reality. This action threatens his marriage to Stella and his friendship with Mitch, who had wanted to marry Blanche before his romanticised view of her was shattered by Stanley.

In *Streetcar*, Williams employs what he himself has referred to as a 'poetic naturalism': the drama is located in the real, but it reaches for the intangible and the poetic. He paints a picture of a society in a state of transition and uncertainty. Blanche is trying to live in an idealised past, but harsh present reality intrudes and destroys her. The graceful world of the Southern plantation, itself a lie, has gone. The reality of post-war America is the brutishness and gracelessness of Stanley and his poker-playing friends, seen from Blanche's point of view at least, although clearly Blanche's sister sees her husband in quite a different light.

As in *Menagerie*, Williams once again employs a range of expressionist theatrical devices: transparent sets, the mixing of theatrical space (the house and the New Orleans street, the bathroom as a symbolic refuge for Blanche), evocative music to create atmosphere and make character points, lighting (for example, the lampshade that Blanche insists on), sound effects and, in particular, a heightened poetic language. Here is a speech of Blanche's near the end of the play:

> I can smell the sea air. The rest of my time I'm going to spend on the sea. And when I die I'm going to die on the sea. You know what I shall die of? I shall die of eating an unwashed grape one day out on the ocean. I will die with my hand in the hand of some nice-looking ship's doctor, a very young one with a blonde moustache and a big silver watch. 'Poor lady,' they'll say, 'the quinine did her no good. The unwashed grape has transported her to heaven.'
>
> *(Scene 11)*

Because Blanche lives in a world of self-delusion, she uses language to protect herself from the harsh reality of her own situation and what she sees as the surrounding crudeness. Williams has her talk in a falsely poetic way and thus subtly communicates her pathetic attempts to disguise her own desperation through her pretentious use of words.

Cat on a Hot Tin Roof (1955)

The success of *Cat on a Hot Tin Roof* was timely, because, after the great success of *The Glass Menagerie* and *A Streetcar Named Desire* on Broadway, Williams had had three plays staged that were comparative failures: *Summer and Smoke* (1948), *The Rose Tattoo* (1951) and *Camino Real* (1953). *Camino Real* is a poetic fantasy using, in part, characters from myth and other fictions (Casanova and Marguerite Gautier – the dying heroine of Alexander Dumas' novel, *The Lady of the Camelias,* and the heroine of Verdi's opera, *La Traviata* – for example) in an undefined setting and with very little dramatic incident or development.

After the failure of *Camino Real*, which he considered was because the play was too challenging for Broadway audiences, Williams decided to have a more realistic setting and a more defined dramatic conflict in his next play. *Cat on a Hot Tin Roof* is set in a big mansion on a plantation in the Mississippi Delta. Big Daddy Pollitt represents the 'new money' of the South; he behaves like a tyrant, even though he is dying of cancer. His main concern is that Brick, one of his sons, an ex-athlete and married to Maggie the Cat, father a child so that the inheritance of the estate can pass through his branch of the Pollitt family rather than go to the 'no-neck monster' children of his other son, Gooper, married to the grasping Mae. Maggie is intent on satisfying Big Daddy's wish for a suitable heir. Brick, however, is resistant to assuming these responsibilities because of his sense of impotence, arising from his unresolved emotional problems connected with the death of a close male friend and his marriage to Maggie the Cat.

One criticism that is sometimes levelled at Williams is that he pandered to audience's wishes to see 'Southern grotesques' represented on stage and screen. Some critics see this as a limitation in Williams. In the pages and plays of writers like the novelists William Faulkner and Carson McCullers – and Williams himself – the South seemed to be full of extreme characters living lives of 'a unique moral perversity'. Certainly 'the South' had a psychological reality for audiences and readers through its representation in novels, plays and films, as well as being a real physical region. Characters who clung to the legends of the old South came into conflict with those who identified themselves with the new money of the reconstructed South. Big Daddy belongs to the latter group and it is his dying wish that Brick perform his duty and pick up his legacy to continue the success of the Pollitt family enterprise.

Other dramatists and plays

William Inge (1913–73) was a very successful playwright in the fifteen years after the war. His four best-known plays are: *Come Back, Little Sheba* (1950), *Picnic* (1953), *Bus Stop* (1955) and *The Dark at the Top of the Stairs* (1957). His plays are set in the mid-West of America and his characters are 'ordinary' people trapped within unsatisfying lives. They seek escape from the humdrum routine of existence through alcohol or marital infidelities. Inge's plays are realist in language, characterisation, theme and setting, which made them easily adaptable to the film medium. All the above four plays were made into films and it was the 'humanity' of the easily recognisable, flawed and ordinary characters that audiences warmed to. Their very ordinariness defines also the limitations of the plays: they smack more of realistic 'slices-of-life' rather than domestic tragedies that affect us deeply.

Carson McCullers (1917–67) is much better known as a novelist than as a dramatist, but she had one major dramatic success that repays study: *The Member of the Wedding* (1957), which she adapted for the stage from her own novel. In the character of Frankie Adams, McCullers manages to evoke theatrically the pain and uncertainties of adolescence. The setting once again is the South and the play focuses on the increasing rebellion of black Americans at being treated as second-class citizens.

An extract from *The Member of the Wedding* appears on pages 84–85.

Lorraine Hansberry (1930–65) had one major success in the theatre during her short life: *A Raisin' in the Sun*. Hansberry was one of the few black American dramatists to break into the white, male-dominated American theatre. Her play concerns the trials of a black family, the Youngers, and their struggle to make for themselves a worthwhile, dignified life in a racial ghetto within a racist society where 'the Man' rules and black people struggle to have justice and equality of opportunity. It comes into the category of the 'well-made play': the conventionally-structured two- or three-act play with familiar themes, characters and dramatic development and resolution. That essentially realistic approach, and possibly the non-militant tone of the piece, helped to make it a success with white audiences of the time. However, it is certainly still worth studying from a historical perspective as a representation of the rise in black consciousness on the eve of the decade when the battle for civil rights in America would reach its height.

Assignments

1 Choose one of the extracts from Part 3 of this book written by any one of the following dramatists: Arthur Miller, Tennessee Williams, Carson McCullers. Discuss the scene in a group, identifying what you think the dramatist was trying to communicate through his or her use of language, setting, action and other means of theatrical expression. Then attempt a staging of the scene, with one person taking on the role of the director and others in the group acting the parts.

   Once you have carried out this staging of the scene, each of the group should write about what this exercise revealed about the scene.

2 As a group, choose one play from this period that you have all enjoyed reading. Discuss what the play meant to you and how much it reflected the American society of its time.

   Then, as individuals, write a piece on the play, identifying what it communicates to you and how it reflected the America of the time.

3 In the 1940s and 1950s, America saw a renewal of the 'Red Scares' that had been a feature of the 1920s and 1930s. Choose one or two plays from

this period that represents dramatically the hysteria and persecution of individuals for 'Un-Americanism'.

4   One of the criticisms made about Arthur Miller's plays is that the concerns of his women characters are made subservient to the male characters. Tennessee Williams, however, frequently made women the central characters of his plays. Choosing at least one female character from one play by both Miller and Williams, show how their representation of women and female concerns was different.

5   Of the American plays of this period that you have read, which one (or two) is the most interesting in the way it represents the racial issues that concerned American society at that time?

6   Choose one play written and performed in this period that you would describe as essentially 'realist' in its approach. Then choose one play from the same period that departs from realism and is more 'expressionist' in language and other ways. Compare the two and say which you find the more interesting approach and why.

7   Of the plays you have read from this period of American drama, which one do you think most vividly reflects the America of its time?

8   What picture of the American South emerges from any of the plays of Tennessee Williams and/or Carson McCullers?

9   Does the term 'social drama' adequately describe Arthur Miller's plays written and performed during this period? How does Miller's dramatic technique develop between *All My Sons* and *Death of a Salesman*?

10 Choose one play from this period that you found particularly interesting and reflective of American society. Then consider a film version of the play (e.g. *A Streetcar Named Desire* in which Marlon Brando played Stanley or the 1997 version of *The Crucible,* which starred Daniel Day-Lewis) and discuss what changes have been made to the play in adapting for the medium of the cinema. You might consider whether the film version has been altered in any way for commercial reasons to please a mass audience or for reasons of moral or political censorship. Discuss also how the play text has been altered to suit the more visual medium of film.

1960–90: fragmented drama in a fragmented society

The historical, social and cultural context

The 1950s is often regarded as a period of relative calm before the storm that broke over American society in the 1960s and 1970s. American dramatists would chronicle the maelstrom that America became in these decades.

When, in 1960, John Kennedy became President, he spoke of a 'New Frontier' that he hoped would challenge Americans. He was trying to invoke the spirit of the American West and its associated myths of fearless pioneers taming the wilderness. However, that 'frontier spirit' had involved depriving Native Americans of lands and rights. In his inaugural speech, Kennedy had implored Americans to 'ask not what your country can do for you, but what you can do for your country'. Despite such rhetoric and high aspirations, Kennedy's brief, 'New Frontier' Presidency would precede a decade or more of deep divisions in American society.

By the end of the decade, the United States had conquered the new frontier of space when in 1969 America's costly space programme was vindicated with the landing of astronauts on the moon's surface. However, the country was by this time involved in the Vietnam War and was racked by internal conflicts. The battle by black Americans for equal rights had intensified. Kennedy's government became deeply embroiled in civil disorders which arose from the struggle for equal rights led by black leaders such as Martin Luther King. It seemed also that many young Americans were alienated from American society and were challenging established values. The struggle for equal rights by women had intensified.

The Cold War had reached crisis in 1962 when President Kennedy objected to the Soviet Union establishing rocket bases in Cuba, now ruled by a Communist regime America perceived as hostile. The world teetered on the edge of nuclear warfare during what came to be known as the 'Cuban Missile Crisis'. Somehow a compromise was reached, but it had been a reminder of how fragile world peace was.

President Kennedy was assassinated in 1963, and Americans found themselves asking how this could happen in the greatest democracy in the world. However, in the next ten years Americans would suffer further blows to their concept of America as a free and just society and were to witness riots in major cities, a rising tide of crime and dependence on drugs, and mass protests against America's involvement in the Vietnam War and the draft. The new President, Lyndon Johnson, talked of shaping a 'Great Society', but major problems of race and gender discrimination, and the increasing alienation of many of America's youth, still confronted the nation.

President Johnson is generally given credit for having achieved more for black

Americans in terms of civil rights than all Kennedy's rhetoric had managed, but the deep divisions in American society were tragically highlighted when the black leaders Martin Luther King and Malcolm X were assassinated. By 1968, when Richard Nixon took over as President, it was acknowledged that America could not 'win' the conflict in Vietnam and the process of extracting American forces from that involvement began. Widespread disturbances on college campuses and at the 1968 Democratic Convention in Chicago caused further fissures in American society. At times, the majority of American youth seemed to be in open revolt against their elders.

That revolt also manifested itself in social trends such as 'hippiedom', 'flower power', and the use of illegal drugs. These signs of rebellion among young Americans affronted 'Middle America', those who believed in the traditional, conservative American values of God, patriotism and who found their spokesman in the conservative Richard Nixon. The Women's Liberation Movement also challenged traditional values, as women battled to have equal rights under the law and to have equal access to education and the job market.

Peace in Vietnam was eventually achieved in 1973, but not before it had inflicted deep and lasting wounds on American society. A year later, President Nixon, who had been re-elected by a massive majority in 1972, had to resign over his involvement in the Watergate affair. The political scandal of Watergate began in late 1972 when it became evident that a break-in at the Washington headquarters of the Democratic Party involved the Nixon administration up to the very highest levels. The revelations of official corruption that Watergate uncovered shook the faith of many Americans in the strength of American democracy and its justice system.

The Ford and Carter administrations (see the Chronology on pages 124–125) that followed could be perceived as trying to heal the divisions that had opened up in society over the previous decade or so. President Carter's Democratic administration was intent on being a peacemaker at home and abroad. In 1980, President Reagan was elected, bringing a new conservatism to government, based on encouraging business interests at the expense of state intervention and promoting the philosophy of self-reliance rather than dependence on social welfare. This led inevitably to conflict with minority groups and organised labour. It was an era where it was pronounced that 'greed is good' and the selling of bonds on the stock exchange reached a new peak.

Reagan's administration also took a hard line on what the President called the 'Evil Empire' controlled by the Soviet Union and Communism. The administration was itself dogged by allegations of misconduct over the illegal funding of right-wing extremists in Latin American countries. It seemed to be partially vindicated when the Soviet Union broke up in disarray, the Berlin Wall fell, and Communist control in Eastern Europe seemed to collapse in the early 1990s. However, many American cities were rife with crime and violent outbursts of the dispossessed, the problem of drug proliferation would not go away, and by no means all Americans were sharing in the prosperity of the 1980s. There seemed to be ever-widening gulfs between the 'haves' in American society and the 'have-nots', many of whom lived in the black and Hispanic communities in big cities such as New York and Los Angeles.

Just as American society during this era seemed to be riven by deep divides, so also did America's cultural life appear to become increasingly divided between a mass, popular culture (movies, pop and rock music, comics, 'best-sellers', Broadway shows) and the 'serious ' arts (literary fiction, art movies, classical music, experimental, off-Broadway theatre and avant-garde art). Many cultural theorists claim that during these decades pop culture became dominant – to the detriment of serious art – with a resultant 'dumbing-down' of cultural standards and the acceptance of the mediocre or the sensational as the norm.

For example, American movies became increasingly dominated by special effects and action spectacle; Broadway was largely given over to lavish musicals or mindless comedies; and the literary novel fought a losing battle against the blockbuster bestseller. Perhaps partly because of this seeming domination of pop culture, American writers and dramatists sought to express themselves in new, less structured forms. If writers were addressing themselves to a smaller and smaller 'informed' audience, then they could safely indulge in experimentation of form and expression, rather than seeking to involve a wider audience with more immediately accessible forms and means of expression. The *Star Wars* movies would be seen by most Americans, whilst the audience for serious theatre and literature shrunk to almost miniscule proportions by comparison.

Arthur Miller and Tennessee Williams

Arthur Miller has continued to write important plays since the 1950s. *After the Fall* (1964) was widely seen as being, in part, about his relationship with the film star, Marilyn Monroe, to whom his marriage had ended in divorce in 1961. However, *After the Fall* is also very much about the Holocaust and the familiar Miller themes of individual and collective guilt and responsibility. *Incident at Vichy* (1964) also deals with the Holocaust and is about the rounding up of Jews in the German-occupied Vichy France. In most of Miller's plays, there seem to be central, objective truths that the playwright is determined to uncover. *The Price* (1968) explores how the past and the present interweave in a drama about family sacrifices, guilts, resentments and illusions, themes that are central to a number of Miller's plays. One of his later plays, *The American Clock* (1980) appeared to employ strongly autobiographical material as Miller returned to the Depression and dramatically traced its impact on a family.

Tennessee Williams' career as a dramatist largely stalled in the 1960s and never really recovered, although his play *Night of the Iguana* won the New York Drama Critics Circle Award in 1961. The central character, an unfrocked priest and sacked tour guide, is living (as do many of Williams' characters) on the edge of disaster, improvising a survival strategy that will enable him to go on living. Tennessee Williams died in 1983.

Edward Albee (1928 –)

Edward Albee is undoubtedly one of the most important playwrights of this period, although his plays are not universally admired. His first successes were with short, one-act plays with small casts: *Zoo Story* (1959), *The Death of Bessie Smith* (1960), *The Sandbox* (1960) and *The American Dream* (1961).

Zoo Story (1959)

Zoo Story is a 'two-hander', a play written to be performed by two actors. The setting is a New York park with a bench at the centre of the action. The encounter is between two strangers: one is a middle-class, white American in his forties, who can be identified as representing conformity in American society; the other is a man in his thirties, who talks and behaves as though he might be unstable. Albee was probably influenced by the plays of Samuel Beckett (*Waiting for Godot*) and British playwright Harold Pinter (*The Birthday Party*) when he wrote *Zoo Story*. The play, like Beckett and Pinter's works, can usefully be classified in the category of the **theatre of the absurd**. Absurdist drama turns reality on its head in order to represent the playwright's own vision of reality and often incorporates some critical comment on society. A feature of absurdist drama is that there is very little dramatic action; in addition, the dramatic figures talk and behave in odd ways. Most 'absurd' plays represent life as meaningless and arbitrary and the relationships between people as very difficult. The 'characters' talk to one another, but real communication is not made. In *Zoo Story*, the two strangers who meet in a park in New York interact in an unconventional way: their words are full of metaphorical rather than literal meaning; there are references to bizarre events. The violent climax to the play seems to emphasise the arbitrary nature of existence.

Here Jerry, the younger of the two male characters of *Zoo Story*, talks about his feeling of loneliness:

> I have gained solitary free passage, if that much further loss can be said to be gain. I have learned that neither kindness nor cruelty by themselves, independent of each other, creates any effect beyond themselves; and I have learned that the two combined, together, at the same time, are the teaching emotion.

Zoo Story represents dramatically the increasing alienation and isolation that many Americans of this period were feeling in the face of a creeping conformity. With its violent ending, it also hints at the growing fear that many American citizens felt about their safety in increasingly violent cities.

The Death of Bessie Smith (1960)

The Death of Bessie Smith deals with a very contemporary issue in American society of this period: racial discrimination and prejudice. The short one-act play takes as its starting point the death of the famous black American blues singer, Bessie Smith. After a car crash, she was refused treatment at a whites-only hospital in America's Deep South and as a result died. Bessie Smith is not actually represented as a character in the action and almost all of the dramatic figures are identified only by their job or status: Nurse, Orderly, Intern, Father. They are intended, it seems, to be recognised as representative white Southern citizens imbued with the kind of racial attitudes that could refuse a badly-injured black woman admittance to a hospital. The racial discrimination represented in the play led to the intensifying of the struggle for civil rights by many black Americans during the 1960s.

The Sandbox (1960) and The American Dream (1961)

The Sandbox and *The American Dream* are linked plays in that three of the characters, Mommy, Daddy and Grandma appear in both. These dramatic figures are again meant to be representative Americans. Albee wrote this in a preface to the published text of *The American Dream*:

> The play is an examination of the American Scene, an attack on the substitution of artificial for real values in our society, a condemnation of complacency, cruelty, emasculation and vacuity; it is a stand against the fiction that everything in this slipping land of ours is peachy-keen.

Albee stressed that the cosy picture of American family life presented by many popular television series and most Hollywood films was false. The ever-increasing consumerism of a mass society was creating a mindless pursuit of wealth and goods that was undermining social values. In both these plays, Albee treats these themes comically, but by calling the second play *The American Dream* he is signalling his intention to strike at the superficiality of much of American life.

▶ Read the extract from *The American Dream* on pages 88–90. Show how Albee satirises the notion of the American Dream in the character of the Young Man, and how the character of Grandma and the words she says undermine the 'peachy-keen' image of American family life.

Who's Afraid of Virginia Woolf? (1963)

Who's Afraid of Virginia Woolf? was Albee's first major commercial success and deals, in part, with the theme of how people need illusions to survive. A warring married couple, George and Martha – the main dramatic figures of the play – sustain between them the illusion that they have a child, but, in fact, they are childless. This is in itself a symbol, perhaps, of the sterility of their lives together. They play sadistic games of mutual humiliation and make targets also of the two younger guests they have invited to their home. Although the play is a comedy, it is intended as a dark comedy, a statement about marriage, moral confusion and cruelty in contemporary America.

Other plays

Tiny Alice (1964) and *A Delicate Balance* (1967) are generally seen as difficult and perhaps wilfully obscure. As the gap widened between serious American drama and Broadway theatre, dominated more and more by musical theatre and light comedies, it was almost as though some dramatists adapted their work more and more for minority consumption and felt free to demand a lot from their audiences.

Sam Shepard (1943 –)

Sam Shepard's plays reflect the influence of pop culture on 'serious' theatre; particular influences on Shepard appear to be Hollywood films, especially westerns, jazz, television, rock music and 'car culture'. In addition, the decay of the Western ideal, or the myths of the American West, are often at the core of his plays.

Shepard's plays resemble absurdist plays with their lack of logical narrative, their departure from **psychological realism**, their 'characters' who behave illogically and the absence of easily identifiable themes and explicit meaning. Yet incidents and actions seem to carry symbolic significance and the figures in the drama play games, enact rituals, sing, act violently and bizarrely. Shepard employs a dramatic language that often sounds like a poetic version of street, Western or 'rock' vernacular. The language draws attention to itself: it is dramatic language as performance, characters using words to create an identity for themselves.

The Tooth of Crime (1972)

Here is an extract from *The Tooth of Crime*, a play that represents the world of the superstars of rock music. A famous disc jockey, Star-Man, is advising the rock star:

This is a tender time. The wrong move'll throw you back a year or more. You can't afford that now. The charts are moving too fast. Every week there's a new star. You don't want to be a fly-by-night mug in the crowd. You want something durable, something lasting. How're you gonna cop an immortal shot if you give up soloing and go into a gang war? They'll rip you up in a night.

(Act 1)

Note the mixture of poetic language ('This is a tender time', 'cop an immortal shot'), American colloquialisms ('a fly-by-night mug in the crowd') and the references to pop culture ('the charts', 'a new star'). *The Tooth of Crime* is a particularly 'raw' play with 'bad' language and explicit scenes, which reflect the world it represents.

True West (1980)

Hollywood and the American West are the main cultural references in Shepard's play *True West*, which deals with sibling rivalries and dysfunctional families. One of the brothers makes his living as a screenwriter for Hollywood, but his rootless brother usurps his role by managing to sell a screenplay of a western to a Hollywood producer. The decay of the American West and the myths associated with the opening-up of the West are central to this play.

Buried Child (1978)

Buried Child deals with a dysfunctional family living on a farm that appears to be non-functional as well. No one seems to communicate with anyone else in this family. The 'buried child' of the play's title may refer to some hidden horror in the family history, or it may refer to the buried child that there is in all of us (a comparison can be made with Albee's use of the imagined child of George and Martha in *Who's Afraid of Virginia Woolf*). Often in Shepard's plays, explicit meaning is absent and it is open to the audience, or readers, to bring their own interpretation to the drama. This is a characteristic of serious contemporary drama: the elusiveness of meaning, which is not the same thing as saying it is without meaning.

The Curse of the Starving Class (1978)

The Curse of the Starving Class seems to refer to the decay of the Western ideal. It represents the usurpation of the land by real estate developers whose only interest is in the building of apartment buildings or shopping malls, not in the growing of crops. In this play Shepard appears to be critical of the rampant materialism and soullessness of much of American life. The American Dream, he appears to say, has been betrayed and people have lost touch with their roots. America is in danger of becoming one sprawling suburb full of shopping opportunities and hideous housing developments.

Fool for Love (1986)

Dysfunctional families are a recurring feature in Shepard's dramas and in *Fool for Love* he represents the passions and hatreds of a brother and sister as they deal with their tortured feelings towards one another. Shepard avoids straightforward psychological realism in representing the characters and substitutes instead a raw expression of emotional and physical violence. *Fool for Love* exemplifies the difficulty of pinpointing exactly what most of Shepard's plays are about, which is not the same thing as saying they are about nothing very much. Certainly, it can be said that they deal with the contemporary American experience and in an oblique way reflect how many Americans lived and felt through the three decades of the 1960s, 1970s and 1980s.

David Mamet (1947–)

David Mamet grew up in Chicago, famous for being the industrial hub of the American mid-West and for its lurid past as the home of notorious gangsters. Mamet is a prolific playwright who is generally accepted, along with Sam Shepard, as one of the two most important dramatists of his generation.

Most of Mamet's plays represent a tough, masculine world of petty crooks, con men, seedy salesmen or eccentrics of one kind or another. The language he writes for his dramatic figures is muscular, tough street slang and frequently obscene. His plays have been criticised for their foul-mouthedness and they are invariably controversial in one way or another. Mamet divides critical opinion between those who admire him for his uncompromising representation of the underbelly of American society and those who think of him as a sensationalist, intent, above all, on shocking audiences.

Mamet acknowledges the British playwright Harold Pinter as an influence on his work: 'It was stuff you heard in the street. It was stuff you overheard in the taxicab. It wasn't writerly.' (Mamet quoted in a *New Yorker* article by John Lahr: see bibliography at the end of Part 4, page 109). By 'writerly', Mamet presumably means literary and artificial. His characters are clearly meant to sound as though they are talking the everyday street language of the times without the literary intervention of the playwright. However, his dialogue is strictly speaking not realistic, because it is self-consciously written as a kind of musical fugue with very definite rhythms. The language has been deliberately shaped and 'scored' by the dramatist. Consider this brief extract from his play *The Old Neighborhood:*

BOB	How long can this go on? Wait a minute. Wait a minute. You should call all ...
JOLLY	... I know ...
BOB	... you should cease ...
JOLLY	... I know ...
BOB	... all meetings, dialogue ...
JOLLY	... but the children ...

(from Scene 1)

The dialogue is skilfully written to allow for 'overlapping' where Jolly comes in 'under' Bob's dialogue, thereby making a point about the contrasting points of view of the two characters. Actors playing these parts have to be attuned to the rhythms of the speech.

American Buffalo (1978)

American Buffalo is set in a Chicago junk shop. The characters are small-time crooks who plan to steal a collection of valuable rare coins. However, their incompetence and distrust of one another foil their attempts. Two main themes perhaps emerge from the play: the need for individuals to belong to, and be accepted by, whatever peer group they aspire to and the way in which this world of petty crime and small-fry 'hoods' imitates the attitudes and practices of American big business. Teach, a small-time crook, talks about 'free enterprise' and the freedom of the individual to do anything he sees fit 'in order to secure his honest chance to make a profit ... The country's founded on this, Don. You know this.' The petty criminals' 'chance to make a profit' involves them in planning a criminal act; Mamet deliberately has his characters ape the language of American business so as to draw a parallel between that world and criminality. The word 'characters' must once again be used with care; Mamet himself denies that he creates 'characters': 'There is no character. There are only lines upon a page.' Mamet writes his dialogue according to definite rhythmic patterns and actors must attend to the 'beat' of the language.

▶ Read the extract from *American Buffalo* on pages 95–97. What are the real concerns of Teach when he is talking to Don? How does Mamet use the rhythms of the dialogue to underline meaning?

Glengarry Glen Ross (1983)

In *Glengarry Glen Ross* the main protagonists are not petty crooks, but salesmen of dubious land and real estate developments. These salesmen are 'con men', attempting to 'sucker' their prey into investing money in projects with little chance of producing a return for the investor. The salesmen are desperate to succeed, not only for the high commission and bonuses they earn, but because success in nailing new investors raises their self-esteem and their status among their salesmen peers. Mamet represents a highly competitive world of shark-like salesmen, bullying and ruthless employers, bemused investor victims and isolated, unfeeling human beings. It is also an all-male world in which the linguistic currency is hard-hitting, sarcastic and competitive obscenities. *Glengarry Glen Ross* is a dramatic fable relevant to America of the 1980s under President Reagan's laissez-faire administration with its emphasis on a market economy in which 'Greed is good' (the super-bond salesman character Gordon Gecko says this in Oliver Stone's 1987 film, *Wall Street*) and fortunes were made and lost in financial speculation, until the stock market crashed in October 1987.

Other dramatists and plays

James Baldwin (1924–67) was primarily a novelist and polemical essayist (e.g. *Another Country, The Fire Next Time)*. In the play *Blues for Mister Charlie* (1964) he represents the injustice and racial discrimination that many black Americans experienced, and their mounting frustration that American society was reluctant to confront this deeply divisive racism. *Blues for Mister Charlie* is full of anger at what the writer sees as the continuing injustices black Americans were suffering and the betrayal of the liberal white establishment to pressurise sufficiently for radical change.

▶ Read the extract from *Blues for Mister Charlie* on pages 86–88. Discuss what the main points of disagreement are between the two characters and how the scene leads to the statement 'All white men are Mister Charlie'.

Arthur Kopit (born 1937) wrote two interesting plays in the 1960s: *Oh Dad, Poor Dad, Mama's Hung You in the Closet and I'm Feelin' So Sad* (1960) and *Indians* (1968). In *Oh Dad, Poor Dad*, he satirises viciously the myth of the average happy American family and specifically the figure of the overbearing, all-devouring Mom. In *Indians* he employs the real-life character of Buffalo Bill Cody to explore the threadbare nature of the myths surrounding the supposedly heroic 'taming' of the American West and the wholesale massacre of Native Americans and their way of life that this involved. Most contemporary reviewers believed that the genocide portrayed in the play was intended as a metaphor for American policy in the Vietnam War. Clive Barnes, the critic, stated that 'it was Mr Kopit's apt and pertinent point that the spirit informing the American action [in the American West] was much the same as that informing the Vietnam War' (from the Introduction to *Indians* in *Best American Plays* 1967–73).

1   Choose one of these extracts from Part 3 of the book: *Blues for Mister Charlie, The American Dream, Indians, Buried Child* or *American Buffalo*. Discuss the scene as a group, deciding what it is about and how a director and actors would approach a performance of the scene. Then assign roles to each member of the group with one person taking on the role of the director. After some rehearsal, stage the scene within any acting space. Then discuss as a group what you gained and learnt from this exercise.

   Afterwards, as individuals, write an account of what happened and what the staging of the scene revealed about it.

2   Albee's *The Death of Bessie Smith*, Baldwin's *Blues for Mister Charlie* and Arthur Kopit's *Indians* all represent dramatically the reality of racism in American society at different times. Analyse how this racism is represented in at least two of these plays and say which play you find more convincing as a reflection of racism in American society and why.

3   Choose two or three of the plays that you have read from this period and say why you think they convincingly reflect important aspects of American society of the time.

4   The theatre of the absurd is a term that evolved to describe a certain kind of drama from the 1950s on. Edward Albee has been called an absurdist playwright, and there may be absurdist elements in the plays of Arthur Kopit and Sam Shepard. How accurately can the term 'absurdist' be applied to any play by these playwrights?

5   How much do you think plays by David Mamet such as *Glengarry Glen Ross* and *American Buffalo* or, indeed, any other play by Mamet, reflect the America of their time? Or is Mamet primarily a playwright concerned more with the individual than with social issues?

6   Which play or plays that you have read from this period represents most vividly the decay of the American Dream?

7   Numerous plays that have been discussed in this section represent family life in some way. Basing your argument on at least two plays by different playwrights, show how family life is represented as being in a state of crisis in American society.

8   Discuss the way women are represented in any two plays of this period and how these representations may reflect the changing status and roles of women in American society.

2 | Approaching the texts

Part 2 examines different ways in which drama texts might be read and interpreted.

- What do the language, 'characters' and sub-text reveal about a play and the intentions of the playwright?

- How do different factors – such as genre, 'historical perspective', a particular staging, the playwright's intentions, the individual experiences of the reader or audience, – influence our interpretation of the meaning of a play?

- How did important movements in the theatre, and in the arts generally, help to shape the writing of the playwrights studied?

Drama as text

There are three possible ways of looking at plays on the printed page:

- plays as a branch of literature, drama as written text
- plays studied 'on the page' but taking into account that the text is intended for performance
- play text as a blueprint for actual performance, the text of the play being used for rehearsal and then performance.

Much insight can be gained about a play's themes and philosophy by studying it on the page and analysing it against the background of the historical, social and cultural context in which it was written. Nevertheless, when you are studying plays as text, always bear in mind that plays are written to be performed and try to consider how the text could be transformed into performance.

The language of drama

Playwrights give their 'characters' words to speak; this dramatic speech is often referred to as dialogue. The writer tries to give each dramatic figure an individual voice that suits the 'character'. An actor playing a particular role has to decide how the character's lines should be delivered: with what kind of accent, intonation, emphasis and tone. After all, the characters in a play cannot all sound exactly like one another, otherwise the illusion that they are separate human individuals would be shattered. Consider this extract from *The Iceman Cometh* by Eugene O'Neill:

LEWIS	(earnestly) My dear fellow, I give you my word of honour as an officer and a gentleman, you shall be paid tomorrow.
WETJOEN	Ve swear it, Harry. Gif him hell!
MCGLOIN	There you are, Harry. Sure, what could be fairer?
MOSHER	Yes, you can't ask for fairer than that, Harry. A promise is a promise as I've often discovered.

(Act 1)

O'Neill differentiates the 'characters' from one another by giving them distinctive 'voices': Lewis with his upper-class style, Wetjoen with his immigrant's American English, McGloin with his American Irish intonation and Mosher with more standard American English.

▶ Read the extract from *The Iceman Cometh* on pages 74–76. What does Larry reveal about himself and his attitudes to the Movement and society in general? What is the atmosphere between the two men and how does O'Neill communicate that through the dialogue?

'Characters'

You will have noticed that when the word 'character' has been used so far, mostly it has been encased in single inverted commas. This has been done to draw your attention to the implications of using the word 'character'. A character in a play is not a real human being, but that is how characters in plays are often discussed. Characters are figures within a drama text created by a writer through words and actions. For example, Hamlet and King Lear are often discussed as though they are real human beings, but Hamlet and King Lear have never existed. They are fictional figures within a dramatic context and created by Shakespeare through language.

Where, then, does this leave students of a drama text? Is it possible for a distancing to take place from the characters and what is read on the page? Is it necessary constantly to bear in mind that these are not real people and that being drawn into empathising with their dramatic situation should be avoided, because that would be giving into the manipulation of the dramatist who has created these 'characters' through language? Or should the aim be to identify with the characters and perceive them as real beings within a real life situation?

A useful illustration of this total identification with 'real' situations and 'real' people can be taken from the world of television soap operas. Long-running soap operas attract millions of loyal viewers who share the trials and tribulations, the joys and sadness, of the regular 'characters' featured in the series. For many people, these characters become as real as real human beings, and some fans will go as far as to write to the characters, sympathising with the problems they are facing. They write to the characters, not the actors playing the roles, because they accept the reality of the life portrayed on the screen to such a degree that they think of the characters as actual human beings – not merely as figures within a long-running dramatic context.

Most of us are drawn into a play when we read it or when we sit in a theatre. There is nothing wrong with that and we will almost certainly gain more from a performance or a reading if we allow ourselves to identify with the situations the 'characters' find themselves in. However, some part of us should always be aware that what we are reading or watching is a fiction, and that these characters are created by a fusion of language and action. By doing this, we can analyse how the characters within a drama are created and reach a clearer understanding of the meaning they embody.

▶ Read the extract from *The Time of Your Life* that appears on pages 72–74. Saroyan's dialogue is more 'elusive' in its meaning than, say, the dialogue Clifford Odets or Arthur Miller writes. Discuss the voice that Saroyan gives to the three characters in this scene and how each actor might say the words to communicate something important about their character to an audience.

Theatrical language

So far in discussing language in the context of drama, we have meant words, dialogue, dramatic speeches. But there is another form of 'language' that dramatists may employ: a theatrical language that has to do with performing a play in a theatre and the use of the theatrical space, theatrical technology and the visual aspects of a performance. Consider these opening stage directions from William Saroyan's *The Time of Your Life*.

An extract from the play appears on pages 72–74.

At the very beginning of the play 'The Missouri Waltz' is coming from the phonograph. The music ends here. This is the signal for the beginning of the play. Joe comes out of his reverie. He whistles the way people do who are calling a cab about a block away, only he does it quietly. Willie turns round, but Joe gestures for him to return to his work. Nick looks up from 'The Racing Form'.

JOE   *(calling)* Tom. *(to himself)* Where the hell is he, every time I need him?
(He looks round calmly: the nickel-in-slot phonograph in the corner; the open public telephone; the stage; the marble-game; the bar and so on. He calls this time very loud.)

In these stage directions, Saroyan is making use of some of the non-verbal theatrical language at his disposal as a dramatist: music on the 'phonograph', sounds the characters make ('whistles'), gestures, actions and props (the phonograph, the horse-racing paper, the marble-game, etc.).

The 'scenery' (the set, if any, and the stage furniture), the objects that decorate the set, sound effects, music, the props the characters handle – all may be used to communicate meaning in the medium of the theatre. In addition, there are the clothes the characters wear, their general appearance, the style in which the action is lit by the person in charge of lighting and the use of the theatrical space. Meaning is communicated by a combination of all these aspects of performance in a theatre. They provide a writer for the theatre with an additional form of language that is non-verbal.

Sub-text

When people talk to one another in real life, the meaning of what they say is often produced not only by the words they speak, but also by what they do not say out loud. Very often conversations may appear on the surface to be about one thing, when they are actually about something quite different. In drama, a skilful playwright can also create a **sub-text** which exists beneath the layer of overt meaning produced by the words the characters are given to speak. What is not being said becomes the real meaning of the exchange of words.

Consider this short extract from Eugene O'Neill's play *The Iceman Cometh*. Two characters, Larry and Parritt, are discussing how a group of revolutionaries came to be arrested by the police.

A longer extract from this play appears on pages 74–76.

LARRY	... I'd swear there couldn't be a yellow stool pigeon among them.
PARRITT	Sure, I'd have sworn that, too, Larry.
LARRY	I hope his soul rots in hell, whoever it is!
PARRITT	Yes, so do I.
LARRY	(after a pause – shortly) How did you locate me? I hoped to have found a place of retirement where no one in the Movement would ever come to disturb my peace.
PARRITT	I found out through Mother.

(Act 1)

The director and actors, in dealing with this piece of dialogue, would somehow have to communicate the sub-text of the exchange between the characters: that

Larry has his suspicions that Parritt is the police informer. O'Neill signals how this sub-text can be represented by his use of the stage direction ('after a pause – shortly'). A dramatic pause or silence can often be used to imply meaning, something that is not being said, but which is very much the real meaning operating 'under the text', as it were.

It is important to be aware of the dramatic device of sub-text and to read texts with a readiness to detect a further layer of meaning beneath the surface meaning.

'Privileging the dramatist'

One of the central aims of this book is to stress the value of viewing plays within the historical, social and cultural framework of the time in which they were written and performed. When plays are revived twenty, thirty or even hundreds of years after they were written, the perspective changes and we usually see them in a different light from how they were initially perceived. **Historical perspective** can alter how the 'meaning' of a play is interpreted. For example, it is over forty years since Arthur Miller's play *The Crucible* received its first performance. Those forty years provide a historical perspective on the play that perhaps allows us to interpret it slightly differently from the audiences who first saw it performed. In the 1950s, audiences would have been intensely aware of the McCarthyite investigations then taking place in America. They would have been able to make a direct connection between the events being enacted on stage and contemporary American history. Present-day audiences have to make that leap of understanding because those particular social and political circumstances no longer exist, but they might make more contemporary connections: the danger of conformist attitudes, for example, in a society that pays lip-service to personal freedoms, but which gives licence to an elected government to dictate how we should live.

However, this raises the question as to what the 'meaning' of any play is. Does the meaning of a drama text stem entirely from the playwright, for example? Is she or he the sole originator of meaning in the drama? Is it the task of a student of the play text to try to figure out what the dramatist is trying to say?

Drama is a collaborative activity. Dramatists cannot produce performances of their plays by themselves: they are dependent on actors, directors and other people to interpret the texts they have written. An actor, for example, can bring to the playing of a part an extra dimension that may not have been foreseen by the dramatist when the play was being written. A **director** can stage the play in such a way that he or she offers an interpretation of the play that may not have been the conscious intention of the dramatist. Indeed, one of the developments in theatre of the 20th century has been the increasing importance of the director in interpreting and communicating meaning in the theatre. Where the director plays just as important a role – or an even more important role – in creating a production of a drama text, then this is often referred to as **directors' theatre**, in which the director of a production supplants the dramatist in terms of the source of meaning. In addition, the audience in a theatre collaborates in the production of meaning, helping by its reactions to the drama to create what the play is about.

Yet, in this book, there is an almost inevitable 'privileging of the dramatist' because we are focusing on plays written by certain American dramatists from different periods of the century. This book involves studying drama texts – although every opportunity should be taken to see these plays performed in a theatre. Inevitably, in taking this approach, the importance of these individual playwrights is emphasised. However, there should be an awareness that not all meaning in a drama text (or in a performance) stems from the writer. Additionally, a dramatist may have had the intention of communicating certain things through the written text, but unconsciously has communicated something quite different to us. There is a term, the **intentionalist fallacy**, that describes this: the fallacy consists of assuming that what the writer intended to communicate becomes the meaning of the text and that we can, in any event, know what the author's intentions were in the first place.

Finally, the meaning of any drama text or any play in performance is not fixed. There is no single meaning that has somehow to be delved out from the text. The text may offer several different interpretations. The meaning each individual ascribes to a play will probably be affected by many factors. For example, one of the extracts used later in this book (see pages 86–88) is a scene from *Blues for Mister Charlie* by James Baldwin, a black American writer whose novels and essays on race reflected his views as a black American living through decades of racial tensions in the States. Inevitably, we will all bring our individual experience and perspectives to interpreting this text, which will be affected by our age, gender, racial background, social class and many other influences. Our view of the play will also be affected by the historical perspective we see it from. What we can offer as individuals is a 'reading' of what the text means to us and that reading will be affected by what we, as individuals, *bring* to the text.

Theatrical genres

Another factor in interpreting meaning in a drama text is the genre of play any individual piece of drama belongs to. **Genre** is a conventional play type, a common kind of drama with its own conventions of theme, characters, settings, language and style. If an analogy with the cinema were to be made, examples of genre films would be westerns, musicals, horror and science fiction movies, comedies and several other types of films that would be easily recognised by cinema-goers as conventional formats. In the theatre, conventional types of plays include detective thrillers, musicals, comedies of various kinds, social-issue plays and tragedies. When a playwright writes a detective play, for example, he or she can draw on the conventions of plot, character and setting that will be familiar to theatregoers who have seen other examples of this genre. The dramatist can follow the conventions of the genre, or she or he can 'subvert' them in some way to create unexpected variations in the conventions of the genre. This can be done by reversing familiar characterisations (for example, the ostensible villain of the piece becomes the most interesting character) or by changing conventional narrative patterns (for example, by substituting an 'unhappy ending' for an expected 'happy ending').

▶ Read the listings pages of a newspaper or magazine to see what shows and plays are being presented in the theatre. Divide the 'shows' into genres, which might include musicals, comedies, classical drama (Shakespeare, for example), thrillers and contemporary social dramas. Do the same for films being shown in your area; genres might include westerns and sci-fi in addition to the theatrical genres already mentioned.

Realism, naturalism and expressionism

Realism was a movement in the theatre that started in the late 19th century and which still shapes much of the contemporary drama we see on our stages, on television and in the cinema. Realism aimed to approximate in dramatic language and situation the problems of everyday life of the times in which plays were performed. Theatrical artificiality, including exaggerated acting styles and 'unrealistic' language, was replaced with an attempt to represent faithfully the lives of the characters the plays were representing. Henrik Ibsen was the first noted realist playwright and his influence spread round the world. (For a discussion of realism see pages 10 and 14, and the following play extracts: *Waiting for Lefty* [pages 67–70], *The Little Foxes* [pages 70–72], *The Iceman Cometh* [pages 74–76], *The Crucible* [pages 81–83] and *Blues for Mister Charlie* [pages 86–88].)

Naturalism was the logical development of realism. In a sense, naturalism is a more extreme form of realism in that it involves an attempt to put real life on stage. Realism produces plays that have clearly defined plots, climaxes and resolutions of the social problems that are represented. Naturalism is not so tied to conventional plotting and resolutions, because, it is argued, life itself does not obey such well-ordered rules. Naturalism could be described usefully as an attempt to put a 'slice-of-life' on stage.

Expressionism is a term that has been used across the arts – in painting, literature and music as well as drama. Expressionist drama is the expression of what dramatists see of the world from within themselves. Expressionist drama does not seek to reproduce ordinary reality, but by theatrical means (heightened language, poetry, visual effects, striking costumes, mime and many other aspects of theatricality) to force an audience to take a fresh look at whatever view of reality is being represented on stage. Eugene O'Neill in his plays *The Emperor Jones* and *The Hairy Ape* and, to a certain extent, Thornton Wilder in *The Skin of Our Teeth* and *Our Town* were influenced by expressionism.

There is an extract from *The Hairy Ape* on pages 59–61.

The alienation effect

Some dramatists choose to destroy an audience's 'suspension of disbelief' by deliberately setting out to remind audiences that what they are watching is not reality, but a performance representing a view of reality. This is sometimes referred to as the **alienation effect**, whereby audiences are 'alienated' from what is happening on stage by being constantly reminded that the dramatic situations and the characters are not real. Suspension of disbelief involves an audience in accepting the illusion that what they are seeing on stage are 'real' events and people. Thus, to break this theatrical illusion, actors sometimes step outside the character they are playing and address the audience directly. Or they are given lines that forcibly remind the audience that they are watching a representation of reality. The point is to destroy the illusion of reality and force the audience to question what is being represented. Audiences are not invited to empathise emotionally with the action or with the characters, so that they can better make a considered judgement about what is being shown to them.

Bertolt Brecht (1898–1956), a German dramatist, is generally credited with successfully employing an alienation technique in the theatre and his influence has affected many writers, including several American dramatists among whom are Clifford Odets and Thornton Wilder. Brecht left Germany in the 1930s after Hitler came to power and spent many years in America, writing plays and screenplays. Brecht and those dramatists whom he influenced wrote plays that largely reject conventional ploys to engage the audience's emotions. Such plays therefore often eschew dramatic incident or continuity, easily recognisable characters, dramatic climaxes, resolutions and explanations.

There is an extract from Odets' *Waiting for Lefty* on pages 67–70.

3 | Play extracts

Eugene O'Neill: *The Hairy Ape* (1922)

Yank is the 'hairy ape' of the title of the play: a man who has been brutalised by the slave labour he has endured shovelling coal into the furnaces of transatlantic liners. Having heard that opposition to the capitalist status quo is led by the International Workers of the World (the IWW or the Wobblies, as they were known), he applies to join the organisation. Organisations like the IWW were viewed with great suspicion by the authorities and frequently infiltrated by the FBI and Pinkerton Agency (a detective agency active against the American labour movement) agents, hence the secretary's suspicions that Yank's naive attitude betrays him as a spy. This scene is written in a realist style, but much of the rest of the play uses expressionist techniques to represent the theme of the dangers of regimentation in American society.

SECRETARY	Only are you sure you understand what you've joined? It's all plain and above board; still, some guys get a wrong slant on us. *(Sharply)* What's your notion of the purpose of the I.W.W.?
YANK	Aw, I know all about it.
SECRETARY	*(sarcastically)* Well, give us some of your valuable information.
YANK	*(cunningly)* I know enough not to speak outa my toin. *(Then resentfully again)* Aw, say! I'm reg'lar. I'm wise to de game. I know yuh got to watch your step wit a stranger. For all youse know, I might be a plain-clothes dick, or somep'n, dat's what yuh're tinkin', huh? Aw, forget it! I belong, see? Ask any guys down to de docks if I don't.
SECRETARY	Who said you didn't?
YANK	After I'm 'nitiated, I'll show yuh.
SECRETARY	*(astounded)* Initiated? There's no initiation.
YANK	*(disappointed)* Ain't there no password – no grip nor nothin'?
SECRETARY	What'd you think this is – the Elks – or the Black Hand?
YANKS	De Elks, hell! De Black Hand, dey're a lot of yellow backstickin' Ginees. Naw. Dis is a man's gang, ain't it?
SECRETARY	You said it! That's why we stand on our own two feet in the open. We got no secrets.

YANK	*(surprised but admiring)* Yuh mean to say yuh always run wide open – like dis?
SECRETARY	Exactly.
YANK	Den yuh sure got your noive wit youse!
SECRETARY	*(sharply)* Just what is it made you want to join us? Come out with that straight.
YANK	Yuh call me? Well, I got noive too! Here's my hand. Yuh wanter blow tings up, don't yuh? Well, dat's me! I belong!
SECRETARY	*(with pretended carelessness)* You mean change the unequal conditions of society by legitimate direct action – or with dynamite?
YANK	Dynamite! Blow it offen de oith – steel – all de cages – all de factories, steamers, buildings, jails – de Steel Trust and all dat makes it go.
SECRETARY	So – that's your idea, eh? And did you have any special job in that line you wanted to propose to us? *(He makes a sign to the men, who get up cautiously one by one and group behind Yank.)*
YANK	*(boldly)* Sure, I'll come out wit it. I'll show youse I'm one of de gang. Dere's dat millionaire guy, Douglas -
SECRETARY	President of the Steel Trust, you mean? Do you want to assassinate him?
YANK	Naw, dat don't get yuh nothin'. I mean blow up de factory, de woiks, where he makes de steel. Dat's what I'm after – to blow up de steel, knock all de steel in the woild up to de moon. Dat'll fix tings! *(Eagerly, with a touch of bravado)* I'll do it by me lonesome! I'll show yuh! Tell me where his woiks is, how to git there, all de dope. Gimme de stuff, de old butter – and watch me do de rest! Watch de smoke and see it move! I don't give a damn if dey nab me – long as it's done! I'll soive life for it – and give 'em de laugh! *(Half to himself)* And I'll write her a letter and tell her de hairy ape done it. Dat'll square tings.
SECRETARY	*(stepping away from YANK)* Very interesting. (He gives a signal. The men, huskies all, throw themselves on YANK and before he knows it they have his legs and arms pinioned. But he is too flabbergasted to make a struggle, anyway. They feel him over for weapons.)*
MAN	No gat, no knife. Shall we give him what's what and put the boots to him?
SECRETARY	No. He isn't worth the trouble we'd get into. He's too

stupid. *(He comes closer and laughs mockingly in YANK's face)* Ho-ho! By God, this is the biggest joke they've put up on us yet. Hey, you Joke! Who sent you – Burns or Pinkerton? No, by God, you're such a bonehead I'll bet you're in the Secret Service! Well, you dirty spy, you rotten agent provocateur, you can go back and tell whatever skunk is paying you blood-money for betraying you're brothers that he's wasting his coin. You couldn't catch a cold.

(Scene 7)

Elmer Rice: *The Adding Machine* (1923)

Rice uses expressionist sets, props, design, 'unrealistic' language and action to represent a critique of contemporary society as he saw it, with its creeping regimentation, the soulless labour that most people had to endure to earn a living and the conformity that was afflicting American society. *The Adding Machine* is very much a modernist drama, not only in its form but in its attack on mass society and its advocacy of escape and individualism. In this scene, Zero and Daisy are represented making their living as automatons. Note the expressionist means by which Rice makes his dramatic points.

SCENE: *an office in a department store. Wood and glass partitions. In the middle of the room, two tall desks back to back. At one desk on a high stool is* ZERO. *Opposite him, at the other desk, also on a high stool, is* DAISY DIANA DOROTHEA DEVORE, *a plain, middle-aged woman. Both wear green eye-shades and paper sleeve-protectors. A pendent electric lamp throws light upon both desks.* DAISY *reads aloud figures from a pile of slips which lie before her. As she reads the figures,* ZERO *enters them upon a large square sheet of ruled paper which lies before him.*

DAISY	*(reading aloud)* Three ninety-eight. Forty-two cents. A dollar fifty. A dollar fifty. A dollar twenty-five. Two dollars. Thirty-nine cents. Twenty-seven fifty.
ZERO	*(petulantly)* Speed it up a little, cancha?
DAISY	What's the rush? Tomorrer's another day.
ZERO	Aw, you make me sick.
DAISY	An' you make me sicker.
ZERO	Go on. Go on. We're losin' time.
DAISY	Then quit bein' so bossy. *(She reads)* Three dollars. Two sixty-nine. Eighty-one fifty. Forty dollars. Eight seventy-five. Who do you think you are, anyhow?

ZERO	Never mind who I think I am. You tend to your work.
DAISY	Aw, don't be givin' me so many orders. Sixty cents. Twenty-four cents. Seventy-five cents. A dollar fifty. Two fifty. One fifty. One fifty. Two fifty. I don't have to take it from you and what's more I won't.
ZERO	Aw, quit talkin'.
DAISY	I'll talk all I want. Three dollars. Fifty cents. Fifty cents. Seven dollars. Fifty cents. Two fifty. Three fifty. Fifty cents. One fifty. Fifty cents.

(She goes bending over the slips and transferring them from one pile to another. ZERO bends over his desk, busily entering the figures.)

ZERO	*(without looking up)* You make me sick. Always shootin' off your face about somethin'. Talk, talk, talk. Just like all the other women. Women make me sick.
DAISY	*(busily fingering the slips)* Who do you think you are, anyhow? Bossin' me around. I don t have to take it from you and what's more I won't.

(They both attend closely to their work, neither looking up.)

ZERO	Women make me sick. They're all alike. The judge gave her six months. I wonder what they do in the workhouse. Peel potatoes. I'll bet she's sore at me. Maybe she'll try to kill me when she gets out. I better be careful. Hello Girl Slays Betrayer. Jealous Wife Slays Rival. You can't tell what a woman's liable to do. I better be careful.
DAISY	I'm gettin' sick of it. Always pickin' on me about somethin'. Never a decent word out of you. Not even the time o' day.
ZERO	I guess she wouldn't have the nerve at that. Maybe she doesn't even know it's me. They didn't even put my name in the paper, the big bums. Maybe she's been in the workhouse before. A bum like that. She didn't have nothin' on that one time – nothin' but a shirt. *(He glances up quickly, then bends over again.)* You make me sick. I'm sick of lookin' at your face.
DAISY	Gee, ain't that whistle ever goin' to blow? You didn't used to be like that. Not even good mornin' or good evenin'. I ain't done nothin' to you. It's the young girls. Goin' round without corsets.
ZERO	Your face is gettin' all yeller. Why don't you put some paint on it? She was puttin' on paint that time. On her cheeks and on her lips. And that blue stuff on her eyes. Just sittin' there in a shimmy puttin' on the paint. An'

	walkin' round the room with her legs all bare.
DAISY	I wish I was dead.
ZERO	I was a goddam fool to let the wife get on to me. She ougta get six months at that. The dirty bum. Livin' in a house with respectable people. She'd be livin' there yet, if the wife hadn't o' got on to me. Damn her!
DAISY	I wish I was dead.
ZERO	You oughta move into that room. It's cheaper than where you're livin' now. I better tell you about it. I don't mean always to be pickin' on you.
DAISY	Gas. The smell of it makes me sick.

(ZERO looks up and clears his throat.)

DAISY	*(looking up startled)* Whatja say?
ZERO	I didn't say nothin'.
DAISY	I thought you did.
ZERO	You thought wrong.

(They bend over their work again.)

(Scene 2)

Ben Hecht and Charles MacArthur: *The Front Page* (1928)

In *The Front Page* Hecht and MacArthur satirised the cynicism and opportunism of the tabloid press of the 1920s, whilst at the same time representing the hysteria about 'reds', anarchists and agitators of one kind or another. In this extract, Walter Burns, the editor of *The Examiner*, a sensationalist tabloid newspaper, advises Hildy Johnson, one of his reporters, about the way to write a report on how the newspaper has captured a dangerous anarchist, Earl Williams. They have hidden Williams in a desk in the press room attached to the prison.

WALTER	It's that three-toed Sheriff I'm worrying about. If he starts sticking his snoot into this ... *(Cudgelling his brain)* I wonder if we could arrest him for anything. *(HILDY has never ceased his typing.)* Did you ever get the dope on that stenographer he seduced?
HILDY	*(over his shoulder)* That was the coroner.
WALTER	Haven't we got *any*thing on him – besides graft?
HILDY	*(thoughtfully)* He's got an idiot kid in the asylum.
WALTER	*(depressed)* I don't see how we can use that against him. *(Brightening)* Wait a minute! Idiot kid. Idiot kid. *(He meditates, then sighs)* No, that's impractical ... *(Approaching HILDY)* What's your lead?
HILDY	*(with authorly pride)* 'While hundreds of Sheriff Hartman's paid gunmen stalked through Chicago

	shooting innocent bystanders, spreading their reign of terror, Earl Williams was lurking less than twenty yards from the Sheriff's office where ...'
WALTER	That's lousy! Aren't you going to mention The Examiner? Don't we take *any* credit?
HILDY	I'm putting that in the second paragraph ...
WALTER	Who the hell's going to read the second paragraph? Ten years I've been telling you how to write a newspaper story – My God, have I got to do everything? Get the story? Write the story?...
HILDY	Listen, you bastard! I can blow better newspaper stories out of my nose than you can write!
WALTER	*(cackling)* 'While hundreds of paid gunmen are out taking a walk ...' God, that stinks! You ought to go back to chasing pictures!
HILDY	Yeah!
WALTER	You were *good* at that!
HILDY	You ungrateful bastard! Who wrote the Fitzgerald confession? Who wrote Ruth Randall's diary? How about the Dayton flood? Even the telegraph operator was crying!
WALTER	All right, then, make me cry now! *(Into phone)* Duffy! Listen, Duffy. What's the name of that religious editor of ours? The fellow with the dirty collar? Sipper what? Well, tell the Revered Sipperly I want to see him right away! ... *(to HILDY)* Do you know what I'm gonna do?
HILDY	Shut up, or I'll throw this typewriter at your head!
WALTER	*(happily)* I'm going to get the Reverend Sipperly to make up a prayer for the City of Chicago – right across the top of the paper!... 'Our Father Who art in Heaven – There were four hundred and twenty-one murders in Chicago last year!' All in religious lingo, see? Eight columns Old English Boldface! The God-damnedest prayer you ever heard ... *(Awed at his own resourcefulness)* Christ, what an idea!
HILDY	You better pray that this desk will float out of the window over the paper.
WALTER	Wait a minute, Hildy ... wait, wait! I got an inspiration! Now take this down just as I say it. *(He yanks a page from the typewriter.)*
HILDY	*(leaping)* Some day you're going to do that, Walter, and I'm gonna belt you in the jaw! You God-damn Know-it-all!
WALTER	*(chanting)* Here's your lead: 'The Chicago Examiner

	again rode to the rescue of the city last night in the darkest hour of her history! *(Lowering his voice)* Earl Williams – Earl Williams, the Bolshevik Tiger, who leaped snarling from the gallows upon the flanks of the city, was captured …'
HILDY	I got you! I got you!

(Act 3)

Maxwell Anderson: *Winterset* (1935)

The Sacco and Vanzetti case had been a notorious event in the 1920s. This trial had taken place at the height of the scares about communists and anarchists plotting against the security of the United States. Maxwell Anderson had already dealt with the case in his earlier play *Gods of the Lightning*, but in *Winterset* he decided to employ dramatic verse, in part, to heighten the dramatic impact. In this extract from the play, Garth expresses the burden of guilt he feels that others have been punished for the crime he committed. Edras, his father, argues that he has to live with his guilt and keep quiet. Miriamne is Garth's 15-year-old sister.

GARTH	Yes, and I'll say it! I was with a gang one time that robbed a pay roll. I saw murder done, and Trock Estrella did it. If that got out I'd go to the chair and so would he – that's why he was here today –
MIRIAMNE	But that's not true –
EDRAS	He says it to frighten you, child.
GARTH	Oh, no I don't! I say it because I've held it in too long. I'm damned if I sit here forever, and look at the door, waiting for Trock with his sub-machine gun, waiting for police with a warrant! – I say I'm damned, and I am, no matter what I do! These piddling scales on a violin – first position, third, fifth, arpeggios in E – and what I'm thinking is Romagna dead for the murder – dead while I sat here dying inside – dead for the thing Trock did while I looked on – and I could have saved him, yes – but I sat here and let him die instead of me because I wanted to live! Well, it's no life, and it doesn't matter who I tell, because I mean to get it over!
MIRIAMNE	Garth, it's not true!

GARTH	I'd take some scum down with me if I died – that'd be one good deed.
Edras	Son, son, you're mad – someone will hear.
GARTH	Then let them hear! I've lived with ghosts too long, and lied too long. God damn you if you keep me from the truth! – *(He turns away.)* Oh, God damn the world! I don't want to die! *(He throws himself down.)*
EDRAS	I should have known. I thought you hard and sullen, Garth, my son. And you were a child, and hurt with a wound that might be healed. – All men have crimes, and most of them are hidden, and many are heavy as yours must be to you. *(GARTH sobs.)* They walk the streets to buy and sell, but a spreading crimson stain tinges the inner vestments, touches flesh, and burns the quick. You're not alone.
GARTH	I'm alone in this.
EDRAS	Yes, if you hold with the world that only those who die suddenly should be revenged. But those whose hearts are cancered, drop by drop in small ways, little by little, till they've borne all they can bear, and die – these deaths will go unpunished, now as always. When we're young we have faith in what is seen, but when we're old we know that what is seen is traced in air and built on water. There's no guilt under heaven, just as there's no heaven, till men believe it – no earth, till men have seen it, and have a word to say this is the earth.
GARTH	Well, I say there's an earth, and I say I'm guilty on it, guilty as hell.
EDRAS	Yet till it's known you bear no guilt at all – unless you wish. The days go by like film, like a long written scroll, a figured veil unrolling out of darkness into fire and utterly consumed. And on this veil, running in sounds and symbols of men's minds reflected back, life flickers and is shadow

                    going towards flame. Only what men can see
                    exists in that shadow. Why must you rise and cry out:
                    That was I, there in the ravelled tapestry,
                    there, in that pistol flash, when the man was killed.
                    I was there, and was one, and am bloodstained!
                    Let the wind
                    and fire take that hour to ashes out of time
                    and out of mind! This thing that men call justice,
                    this blind snake that strikes men down in the dark,
                    mindless with fury, keep your hand back from it,
                    pass by in silence – let it be forgotten, forgotten!
                    Oh, my son, my son – have pity!

MIRIAMNE   But if it was true
                    and someone died – then it was more than shadow –
                    and it doesn't blow away –

GARTH   Well, it was true.

EDRAS   Say it if you must. If you have heart to die,
                    say it, and let them take what's left – there was little
                    to keep, even before –

GARTH   Oh, I'm a coward –
                    I always was. I'll be quiet and live. I'll live
                    even if I have to crawl. I know.
                    (He gets up and goes into the inner room.)

MIRIAMNE   Is it better
                    to tell a lie and live?

EDRAS   Yes, child, It's better.

MIRIAMNE   But if I had to do it –
                    I think I'd die.

EDRAS   Yes, child, because you're young.

MIRIAMNE   Is that the only reason?

EDRAS   The only reason.

                                                    (Act 1, Scene 2)

Clifford Odets: *Waiting for Lefty* (1935)

Many of the productions of the Group Theatre (see page 19) in the 1930s were
considered to be examples of 'agit-prop' theatre, that is, plays that preached a
particular political message and aimed to rouse audiences to direct political action.
Waiting for Lefty is one of the best-known examples of this polemical kind of
theatre. It is based on an actual strike by cab drivers in New York. Here Agate
harangues the union members to strike and accuses the union leaders of being in
the pay of the bosses.

AGATE	LADIES AND GENTLEMEN, and don't let anyone tell you we ain't got some ladies in this sea of upturned faces! Only they're wearin' pants. Well, maybe, I don't know a thing; maybe I fell outa the cradle when I was a kid and ain't been right since – you can't tell!
VOICE	Sit down, cockeye!
AGATE	Who's paying you for those remarks, Buddy? – Moscow Gold? Maybe I got a *glass* eye, but it come from working in a factory at the age of eleven. They hooked it out because they didn't have a shield on the works. But I wear it like a medal, cause it tells the world where I belong – deep down in the working class! We had delegates in the union there – all kinds of secretaries and treasurers ... walking' delegates, but not with blisters on their feet! Oh, no! On their fat little ass from sitting on cushions and taking in mazuma. *(SECRETARY and GUNMAN remonstrate in words and actions here.)* Sit down, boys. I'm just sayin' that about unions in general. I know it ain't true here! Why no, our officers is all aces. Why I seen our own secretary Fatt walk outa his way not to step on a cockroach. No, boys, don't think –
FATT	*(breaking in)* You're out of order!
AGATE	*(to audience)* Am I outa order?
ALL	No, no. Speak. Go on, etc.
AGATE	Yes, our officers is all aces. But I'm a member here – and no experience in Philly either! Today I couldn't wear my union button. The damnedest thing happened. When I take the old coat off the wall, I see she's smoking. I'm a sonovagun if the old union button isn't on fire! Yep, the old celluloid was makin' the most god-awful stink: the landlady came up and gave me hell! You know what happened? That old union button just blushed itself to death! Ashamed! Can you beat it?
FATT	Sit down, Keller! Nobody's interested!
AGATE	Yes, they are!
GUNMAN	Sit down like he tells you!
AGATE	*(continuing to audience)* And when I finish ...

(His speech is broken by FATT and GUNMAN who physically handle him. He breaks away and gets to the other side of the stage. The two are about to make for him when some of the committee men come forward and get in between the struggling parties. AGATE's shirt has been torn.)

AGATE	*(to audience)* What's the answer, boys? The answer is, if

we're reds because we wanna strike, then we take over their salute too! Know how they do it? *(makes Communist salute)* What is it? An uppercut! The good old uppercut to the chin! Hell, some of us boys ain't even got a shirt to our back. What's the boss class tryin' to do – make a nudist colony outa of us?

(The audience laughs and suddenly AGATE comes to the middle of the stage so that the other cabmen back him up in a strong clump.)

AGATE   Don't laugh! Nothin's funny! This is your life and mine! It's skull and bones every incha the road! Christ, we're dyin' by inches! For what? For the debutant-ees to have their sweet comin' out parties at the Ritz! Poppa's got a daughter she's gotta get her picture in the papers. Christ, they make 'em with our blood. Joe said it. Slow death or fight. It's war! *(Throughout this whole speech AGATE is backed up by the other six workers, so that from their activity it is plain that the whole group of them are saying these things. Several of them may take alternate lines out of this last long speech.)*

You, Edna, God love your mouth! Sid and Florrie, the other boys, Old Doc Barnes – fight with us for right! It's war! Working class, unite and fight! Tear down the slaughterhouse of our old lives! Let freedom really ring. These slick slobs stand here telling us about bogeymen. That's a new one for the kids – the reds is bogeymen! But the man who got me food in 1932, he called me Comrade! The one who picked me up where I bled, he called me Comrade too! What are we waiting for ... Don't wait for Lefty! He might never come. Every minute – *(This is broken into by a man who has dashed up the centre aisle from the back of the house. He runs up on stage, says)*

MAN   Boys, they just found Lefty!
OTHERS   What? What? What?
SOME   Shhh ... Shhh ...
MAN   They found Lefty ...
AGATE   Where?
MAN   Behind the car barns with a bullet in his head.
AGATE   *(crying)* Hear it, boys, hear it? Hell, listen to me! Coast to coast! HELLO AMERICA! HELLO. WE'RE STORMBIRDS OF THE WORKING CLASS. WORKERS OF THE WORLD ... OUR BONES AND BLOOD! And when we die they'll know what we did to make a new world!

	Christ, cut us up to little pieces. We'll die for what is right! Put fruit trees where our ashes are! *(To audience)* Well, what's the answer?
ALL	STRIKE!
AGATE	LOUDER!
ALL	STRIKE!
AGATE AND OTHERS	*(on stage)* AGAIN!
ALL	STRIKE, STRIKE STRIKE!!!

(Scene 7)

Lillian Hellman: *The Little Foxes* (1939)

The influence of Ibsen on Hellman's plays is clear; she wrote social dramas with strong plots and characters. *The Little Foxes* is perhaps her best-known and most often performed play. The play's setting is the American South around the turn of the 20th century. The Hubbards represent the new breed of Southern capitalist that emerged after the defeat of the Confederacy in the American Civil War. In this extract from the play, they are explaining the South to a Northern businessman, Marshall, whom they hope to persuade to back their business ventures. Ben, Oscar and Regine are brothers and sister, Birdie (a representative of decayed Southern aristocracy) is married to Oscar, and Leo is their son.

MARSHALL	It's very remarkable how you Southern aristocrats have kept together. Kept together and kept what belonged to you.
BEN	You misunderstand, sir. Southern aristocrats have *not* kept together and have *not* kept what belonged to them.
MARSHALL	*(laughs, indicates room)* You don't call this keeping what belongs to you?
BEN	But we are not aristocrats. *(Points to BIRDIE at the piano)* Our brother's wife is the only one of us who belongs to the Southern aristocracy.
(BIRDIE looks towards BEN.)	
MARSHALL	*(smiles)* My information is that you people have been here, and solidly here, for a long time.
OSCAR	And so we have. Since our great-grandfather.
BEN	*(smiles)* Who was *not* an aristocrat, like Birdie's.
MARSHALL	*(a little sharply)* You make great distinctions.
BEN	Oh, they have been made for us. And maybe they are important distinctions. *(Leans forward intimately)* Now

	you take Birdie's family. When my great-grandfather came here, they were the highest-tone plantation owners in this state.
LEO	*(steps to MARSHALL. Proudly)* My mother's grandfather was *governor* of the state before the war.
OSCAR	They owned the plantation, Lionnet. You may have heard of it, sir?
MARSHALL	*(laughs)* No, I've never heard of anything but brick houses on a lake, and cotton mills.
BEN	Lionnet in its day was the best cotton land in the South. It still brings us in a fair crop. Ah, they were great days for those people – even when I can remember. They had the best of everything. *(BIRDIE turns to them)* Cloth from Paris, trips to Europe, horses you can't raise any more, niggers to lift their fingers –
BIRDIE	*(suddenly)* We were good to our people. Everybody knew that. We were better to them than – *(MARSHALL looks up at BIRDIE)*
REGINA	Why, Birdie. You aren't playing.
BEN	But when the war comes these fine gentlemen ride off and leave the cotton, *and* the women, to rot.
BIRDIE	My father was killed in the war. He was a fine soldier, Mr Marshall. A fine man.
REGINA	Oh, certainly, Birdie. A famous soldier.
BEN	*(to BIRDIE)* But that isn't the tale I'm telling Mr Marshall. *(To MARSHALL)* Well, sir, the war ends. Lionnet is almost ruined and the sons finish ruining it. And there were thousands like them. Why? Because the Southern aristocrat can adapt himself to nothing. Too high-tone to try.
MARSHALL	Sometimes it is difficult to learn new ways. *(BIRDIE and ALEXANDRA begin to play. MARSHALL leans forward, listening.)*
BEN	Perhaps, perhaps. *(He sees that Marshall is listening to the music. Irritated, he turns to BIRDIE and ALEXANDRA at the piano, then back to MARSHALL.)* You're right, Mr Marshall. It is difficult to learn new ways. But maybe that's why it's profitable. *Our* grandfather and *our* father learned the new ways and learned how to make them pay. They work. *(Smiles nastily) They* are in trade. Hubbard Sons, Merchandise. Others, Birdie's family, look down on them. To make a long story short, Lionnet now belongs to *us*. *(BIRDIE stops playing.)* Twenty years

ago we took over their land, their cotton and their
daughter.

(Act 1)

William Saroyan: *The Time of Your Life* (1940)

Saroyan belongs to no easily defined category, although his plays are definitely
modernist in sensibility. He lauds eccentric individuality and is against authority,
but there are no clear political attitudes in *The Time of Your Life*, his most enduring
play. Instead, an inherent faith in the goodness of human beings and the potential
for joy in life and in American society shine through. The setting is Nick's Saloon in
San Francisco, a waterfront 'honky-tonk'. The year is 1939. Joe is obviously
slumming it in this down-market drinking den; Kitty is a prostitute and Nick is the
young Italian-American barman who has a crude tattoo on his arm.

JOE	What's the dream, now?
KITTY	What dream?
JOE	What dream! The dream you're dreaming.
NICK	Suppose he did bring you a watermelon? What the hell would you do with it?
JOE	*(irritated)* I'd put it on this table. I'd look at it. Then I'd eat it. What do you *think* I'd do with it, sell it for a profit?
NICK	How should I know what *you'd* do with *anything*? What I'd like to know is, where do you get your money from? What work do you do?
JOE	*(looking at KITTY)* Bring us a bottle of champagne.
KITTY	Champagne?
JOE	*(simply)* Would you rather have something else?
KITTY	What's the big idea?
JOE	I thought you might like some champagne. I myself am very fond of it.
KITTY	Yeah, but what's the big idea? You can't push *me* around.
JOE	*(gently but severely)* It's not in my nature to be unkind to another human being. I have only contempt for wit. Otherwise I might say something obvious, therefore cruel, and perhaps untrue.
KITTY	You be careful what you think about me.
JOE	*(slowly, not looking at her)* I have only the noblest thoughts for both your person and your spirit.
NICK	What are you talking about?

KITTY	You shut up. You –
JOE	He owns this place. He's an important man. All kinds of people come to him looking for work. Comedians. Singers. Dancers.
KITTY	I don't care. He can't call me names.
NICK	All right, sister. I know how it is with a two-dollar whore in the morning.
KITTY	*(furiously)* Don't you dare call me names. I used to be in burlesque.
NICK	If you were ever in burlesque, I used to be Charlie Chaplin.
KITTY	*(angry and a little pathetic)* I *was* in burlesque. I played the burlesque circuit from coast to coast. I've had flowers sent to me by European royalty. I've had dinner with young men of wealth and social position.
NICK	You're dreaming.
KITTY	*(to JOE) I was in burlesque.* Kitty Duval. That was my name. Life-size photographs of me in costume in front of burlesque theaters all over the country
JOE	*(gently, coaxingly)* I believe you. Have some champagne.
NICK	*(going to table, with champagne and glasses)* There he goes again.
JOE	Miss Duval?
KITTY	*(sincerely, going over)* That's not my *real* name. That's my *stage* name.
JOE	I'll call you by your stage name.
NICK	*(pouring)* All right, sister, make up your mind. Are you going to have champagne with him or not?
JOE	Pour the lady some wine.
NICK	OK, Professor. Why you come to this joint instead of one of the high-class dumps uptown is more than I can understand. Why don't you have champagne at the St. Francis? Why don't you drink with a lady?
KITTY	*(furiously)* Don't you call me names – you dentist.
JOE	Dentist?
NICK	*(amazed, loudly)* What kind of cussing is that? *(Pause. looking at KITTY, then at JOE, bewildered)* This guy doesn't belong here. The only reason I've got champagne is because *he* keeps ordering it all the time. Don't think you're the only one he drinks champagne with. He drinks with *all* of them. He's crazy or something.

JOE	*(confidentially)* Nick, I think you're going to be all right in a couple of centuries.
NICK	I'm sorry, I don't understand your English. *(JOE lifts his glass. KITTY slowly lifts hers, not quite sure of what's going on.)*
JOE	*(sincerely)* To the spirit, Kitty Duval.
KITTY	*(beginning to understand and very grateful, looking at him.)* Thank you.

(Act 1)

Eugene O'Neill: *The Iceman Cometh* (1946)

This play was written in 1939, but first performed in 1946, only seven years before the playwright's death. O'Neill is intent on representing how fragile his characters' hold on reality is and how desperately they need their illusions to continue living. The character of Larry appears to represent O'Neill's own views: Larry is a former political activist, but has moved to New York from the West Coast because he has become disillusioned with 'the Movement'. Parritt is the son of a former lover of Larry's, who has just been arrested for her political activities, the victim, it appears, of a betrayal by one of the members of 'the Movement' itself.

PARRITT	It's funny Mother kept in touch with you for so long. When she's finished with anyone, she's finished. She's always been proud of that. And you know how she feels about the Movement. Like a revivalist preacher about religion. Anyone who loses faith in it is more than dead to her; he's a Judas who ought to be boiled in oil. Yet she seemed to forgive you.
LARRY	*(sardonically)* She didn't, don't worry. She wrote to denounce me and try to bring the sinner to repentance and a belief in the One True Faith again.
PARRITT	What made you leave the Movement, Larry? Was it on account of Mother?
LARRY	*(starts)* Don't be a damned fool! What the hell put that in your head?
PARRITT	Why nothing – except I remember what a fight you had with her before you left.
LARRY	*(resentfully)* Well, if you do, I don't. That was eleven years ago. You were only seven. If we did quarrel, it was because I told her I'd become convinced that the Movement was only a beautiful pipe dream.
PARRITT	*(with a strange smile)* I don't remember it that way.

LARRY	Then you can blame your imagination and forget it. (*He changes the subject abruptly*) You asked me why I quit the Movement. I had a lot of good reasons. One was myself, and another was my comrades, and the last was the breed of swine called men in general. For myself, I was forced to admit, at the end of thirty years' devotion to the Cause, that I was never made for it. I was born condemned to be one of those who has to see all sides of a question. When you're damned like that, the questions multiply for you until in the end it's all question and no answer. As history proves, to be a worldly success at anything, especially revolution, you have to wear blinkers like a horse and see only straight in front of you. You have to see, too, that this is all black, and that is all white. As for my comrades in the Great Cause, I felt as Horace Walpole did about England, that he could love it if it weren't for the people in it. The material the ideal free society must be constructed from is men themselves and you can't build a marble temple out of a mixture of mud and manure. When man's soul isn't a sow's ear, it will be time enough to dream of silk purses. (*He chuckles sardonically – then irritably as if suddenly provoked at himself for talking so much*) Well, that's why I quit the Movement, if it leaves you any wiser. At any rate, you see it had nothing to do with your mother.
PARRITT	(*smiles almost mockingly*) Oh sure, I see. But I'll bet Mother has always thought it was on her account. You know her, Larry. To hear her go on sometimes, you'd think she was the Movement.
LARRY	(*stares at him, puzzled and repelled – sharply*) That's a hell of a way for you to talk, after what happened to her!
PARRITT	(*at once confused and guilty*) Don't get me wrong. I wasn't sneering, Larry. Only kidding. I've said the same thing to her lots of times to kid her. But you're right. I know I shouldn't now. I keep forgetting she's in jail. It doesn't seem real. I can't believe it about her. She's always been so free. I – . But I don't want to think about it. (*LARRY is moved to a puzzled pity in spite of himself. PARRITT changes the subject*) What have you been doing all the years since you left – the Coast, Larry?
LARRY	(*sardonically*) Nothing I could help doing. If I don't believe in the Movement, I don't believe in anything else either, especially not the State. I've refused to become a

useful member of its society. I've been a philosophical drunken bum and proud of it. *(Abruptly his tone sharpens with resentful warning)* Listen to me. I hope you've deduced that I've my own reason for answering the impertinent questions of a stranger, for that's all you are to me. I have a strong hunch you've come here expecting something of me. I'm warning you, at the start, so there'll be no misunderstanding, that I've nothing left to give, and I want to be left alone, and I'll thank you to keep yourself to yourself. I feel you're looking for some answer to something. I have no answers to give to anyone, not even myself. Unless you call what Heine wrote in his poem to morphine an answer. *(He quotes a translation of the closing couplet sardonically)*

'Lo, sleep is good; better is death; in sooth, the best of all were never to be born.'

(Act 1)

Tennessee Williams: *A Streetcar Named Desire* (1947)

Set in New Orleans just after the end of the Second World War, *Streetcar* represents what Williams saw as the increasing coarsening of American life and the lack of a caring quality in the way society dealt with its more vulnerable members. In this extract from the play, the sensitive and vulnerable Blanche is preparing to leave the home of her sister. Her sister is married to Stanley, a brutish man who sees through Blanche's pretensions and affectations and resents the genteel airs she affects.

BLANCHE	When I think of how divine it's going to be to have such a thing as privacy once more – I could weep with joy!
STANLEY	This millionaire from Dallas is not going to interfere with your privacy any?
BLANCHE	It won't be the sort of thing you have in mind. This man is a gentleman and he respects me. *(Improvising feverishly)* What he wants is my companionship. Having great wealth sometimes makes people lonely! A cultivated woman, a woman of intelligence and breeding, can enrich a man's life – immeasurably! I have those things to offer, and this doesn't take them away. Physical beauty is passing. A transitory possession. But beauty of the mind and richness of the spirit and tenderness of the heart – and I have all of those things –

	aren't taken away, but grow! Increase with the years! How strange that I should be called a destitute woman! When I have all the treasures locked in my heart. (*A choked sob comes from her*) I think of myself as a very, very rich woman! But I have been foolish – casting my pearls before swine!
STANLEY	Swine, huh?
BLANCHE	Yes, swine! Swine! And I'm thinking not only of you but your friend, Mr Mitchell. He came to see me tonight. He dared to come here in his work-clothes. And to repeat slander to me, vicious stories that he had gotten from you. I gave him his walking papers …
STANLEY	You did, huh?
BLANCHE	But then he came back. He returned with a box of roses to beg my forgiveness! He implored my forgiveness. But some things are not forgivable. Deliberate cruelty is not forgivable. It is the one unforgivable thing in my opinion and it is the one thing of which I have never, never been guilty. And so I told him, I said to him, 'Thank you', but it was foolish of me to think that we could ever adapt ourselves to each other. Our ways of life are too different. Our attitudes and backgrounds are too incompatible. We have to be realistic about such things. So farewell, my friend! And let there be no hard feelings …
STANLEY	Was this before or after the telegram from the Texas millionaire?
BLANCHE	What telegram? No! No, after! As a matter of fact, the wire came just as –
STANLEY	As a matter of fact there wasn't no wire at all!
BLANCHE	Oh, oh!
STANLEY	There isn't no millionaire! And Mitch didn't come back with roses 'cause I know where he is –
BLANCHE	Oh!
STANLEY	There isn't a goddam thing but imagination!
BLANCHE	Oh!
STANLEY	And lies and conceit and tricks!
BLANCHE	Oh!
STANLEY	And look at yourself! Take a look at yourself in that worn-out Mardi Gras outfit, rented for fifty cents from some rag-picker! And with the crazy crown on! What queen do you think you are?
BLANCHE	Oh, God!

STANLEY	I've been on to you from the start! Not once did you pull any wool over this boy's eyes. You come in here and you sprinkle the place with powder and spray perfume and cover the light-bulb with a paper lantern, and lo and behold the place has turned into Egypt and you are the Queen of the Nile. Sitting on your throne and swilling down my liquor! I say – *Ha! Ha!* Do you hear me? *Ha-ha-ha!*

(Scene 10)

Arthur Miller: *Death of a Salesman* (1949)

With the production of *Death of a Salesman* in New York in 1949, Arthur Miller was established as America's leading playwright of his generation. Fusing social drama with techniques drawn from expressionist theatre (e.g. the mingling of present dramatic time with events from the past and the memories of those events as seen from the viewpoint of the main characters, a non-naturalistic use of stage space, non-realistic sets, evocative use of voice and music), Miller created a modern tragedy about a representative American, an 'everyman', in the dramatic figure of a salesman, Willy Loman. All his life Willy has chased the fruits of the American Dream (wealth, status, social acceptance, the perfect family and social life, the control of his own destiny) only to find that the economic system that has exploited his labour is finally only interested in how much profit he can deliver and not in him as a valued individual employee and human being.

In this extract from the play, Willy, by now nearing retirement and exhausted by his efforts and failures, begs Howard, his young employer, for one last chance to re-establish himself and find the success that has always eluded him.

WILLY	I tell ya, Howard. The kids are all grown up, y'know. I don't need much any more. If I could take home – well, sixty-five dollars a week, I could swing it.
HOWARD	Yeah, but Willy, see I –
WILLY	I tell ya why, Howard. Speaking frankly and between the two of us, y'know – I'm just a little tired.
HOWARD	Oh, I understand that, Willy. But you're a road man, Willy, and we do a road business. We've only got a half-dozen salesmen on the floor here.
WILLY	God knows, Howard, I never asked a favor of any man. But I was with the firm when your father used to carry you in here in his arms.
HOWARD	I know that, Willy, but –

WILLY	Your father came to me the day you were born and asked me what I thought of the name of Howard, may he rest in peace.
HOWARD	I appreciate that, Willy, but there just is no spot here for you. If I had a spot I'd slam you right in, but I just don't have a single solitary spot.
	(He looks for his lighter. Willy has picked it up and gives it to him. Pause.)
WILLY	*(with increasing anger)* Howard, all I need to set my table is fifty dollars a week.
HOWARD	But where am I going to put you, kid?
WILLY	Look, it isn't a question of whether I can sell merchandise, is it?
HOWARD	No, but it's a business, kid, and everybody's gotta pull his own weight.
WILLY	*(desperately)* Just let me tell you a story, Howard –
HOWARD	'Cause you gotta admit, business is business.
WILLY	*(angrily)* Business is definitely business, but just listen for a minute. You don't understand this. When I was a boy – eighteen, nineteen – I was already on the road. And there was a question in my mind as to whether selling had a future for me. Because in those days I had a yearning to go to Alaska. See, there were three gold strikes in one month in Alaska, and I felt like going out. Just for the ride, you might say.
HOWARD	*(barely interested)* Don't say.
WILLY	Oh, yeah, my father lived many years in Alaska. He was an adventurous man. We've got quite a little streak of self-reliance in our family. I thought I'd go out with my older brother and try to locate him, and maybe settle in the North with the old man. And I was almost decided to go, when I met a salesman in the Parker House. His name was Dave Singleman. And he was eighty-four years old, and he'd drummed merchandise in thirty-one states. And old Dave, he'd go up to his room, y'understand, put on his green velvet slippers – I'll never forget – and pick up his phone and call the buyers, and without ever leaving his room, at the age of eighty-four, he made his living. And when I saw that, I realised that selling was the greatest career a man could want. 'Cause what could be more satisfying than to be able to go, at the age of eighty-four, into twenty or thirty different cities, and pick up a phone, and be

remembered and loved and helped by so many different people? Do you know? when he died – and by the way he died the death of a salesman, in his green velvet slippers in the smoker of the New York, New Haven and Hartford, going into Boston – where he died, hundreds of salesmen and buyers were at his funeral. Things were sad on a lotta trains for months after that. *(He stands up. Howard has not looked at him)* In those days there was personality in it, Howard. There was respect, and comradeship, and gratitude in it. Today, it's all cut and dried, and there's no chance for bringing friendship to bear – or personality. You see what I mean? They don't know me any more.

HOWARD	*(moving away, to the right)* That's just the thing, Willy.
WILLY	If I had forty dollars a week – that's all I'd need. Forty dollars, Howard.
HOWARD	Kid I can't take blood from a stone, I –
WILLY	*(desperation is on him now)* Howard, the year Al Smith was nominated, your father came to me and –
HOWARD	*(starting to go off)* I've got to see some people, kid.
WILLY	*(stopping him)* I'm talking about your father! There were promises made across this desk! You mustn't tell me you've got people to see – I put thirty-four years into this firm, Howard, and now I can't pay my insurance! You can't eat the orange and throw the peel away – a man is not a piece of fruit! *(After a pause)* Now pay attention. Your father – in 1928 I had a big year. I averaged a hundred and seventy dollars a week in commissions.
HOWARD	*(impatiently)* Now, Willy, you never averaged –
WILLY	*(banging his hand on the desk)* I averaged a hundred and seventy dollars a week in the year of 1928; and your father came to me – or rather, I was in the office here – it was right over this desk – and he put his hand on my shoulder –
HOWARD	*(getting up)* You'll have to excuse me, Willy. I gotta see some people. Pull yourself together. *(Going out)* I'll be back in a little while.

(Act 1)

AMERICAN DRAMA 1900–1990

Arthur Miller: *The Crucible* (1953)

Miller's play is set in 17th century Massachusetts and represents actual events from that era, but it was written with very contemporary issues in mind. Miller himself became the target for the McCarthyite 'witch hunts' of the 1950s (see page 28) when many ordinary American citizens, as well as writers, actors and other artists, were investigated for their past and present connections with communism. In *The Crucible*, Miller illustrates the hysteria that can be whipped up by ambitious people who want to gain power by filling citizens full of fear about 'traitors' in their midst, in this case, so-called witches who have been consorting with the devil. In this extract from the play, Hale (who has come to Salem to investigate witchcraft) is interrogating Tituba, a servant, about a group of young girls who supposedly 'danced with the devil'.

HALE	You would be a good Christian woman, would you not, Tituba?
TITUBA	Aye, sir, a good Christian woman.
HALE	And you love these little children?
TITUBA	Oh, yes, sir, I don't desire to hurt little children.
HALE	And you love God, Tituba?
TITUBA	I love God with all my bein'.
HALE	Now in God's holy name –
TITUBA	Bless Him. Bless Him. *(She is rocking on her knees, sobbing in terror)*
HALE	And to His glory –
TITUBA	Eternal glory. Bless Him – bless God ...
HALE	Open yourself, Tituba – open yourself and let God's holy light shine on you.
TITUBA	Oh, bless the Lord.
HALE	When the Devil comes to you, does he ever come – with another person? *(She stares up into his face.)* Perhaps another person in the village? Someone you know.
PARRIS	Who came with him?
PUTNAM	Sarah Good? Did you ever see Sarah Good with him? Or Osburn?
PARRIS	Was it man or woman came with him?
TITUBA	Man or woman. Was – was woman.
PARRIS	What woman? A woman, you said. What woman?
TITUBA	It was black dark, and I –
PARRIS	You could see him, why could you not see her?

TITUBA	Well, they was always talking; they was always runnin' round and carryin' on –
	(Now HALE takes her hand. She is surprised)
HALE	Tituba. You must have no fear to tell us who they are, do you understand? We will protect you. The devil can never overcome a minister. You know that, do you not?
TITUBA	*(kisses HALE's hand)* Aye, sir, oh, I do.
HALE	You have confessed yourself to witchcraft, and that speaks a wish to come to Heaven's side. And we will bless you, Tituba.
TITUBA	*(deeply relieved)* Oh, God bless you, Mr Hale!
HALE	*(with rising exaltation)* You are God's instrument put in our hands to discover the Devil's agents among us. You are selected, Tituba, you are chosen to help us cleanse our village. So speak utterly, Tituba, turn your back on him and face God – face God, Tituba, and God will protect you.
TITUBA	*(joining with him)* Oh, God, protect Tituba!
HALE	*(kindly)* Who came to you with the Devil? Two? Three? Four? How many?
(TITUBA pants, and begins rocking back and forth again, staring ahead.)	
TITUBA	There was four. There was four.
PARRIS	*(pressing in on her)* Who? Who? Their names, their names!
TITUBA	*(suddenly bursting out)* Oh, how many times he bid me kill you, Mr Parris!
PARRIS	Kill me!
TITUBA	*(in a fury)* He say Mr Parris must be kill! Mr Parris no godly man, Mr Parris mean man and no gentle man, and he bid me rise out of my bed and cut your throat! *(They gasp)* But I tell him 'No! I don't hate that man. I don't want kill that man.' But he say, 'You work for me, Tituba, and I make you free! I give you pretty dress to wear, and put you way up high in the air, and you gone fly back to Barbados!' And I say, 'You lie, Devil, you lie!' And then he come one stormy night to me and he say, 'Look! I have *white* people belong to me. And I look – and there was Goody Good.
PARRIS	Sarah Good!
TITUBA	*(rocking and weeping)* Aye, sir, and Goody Osburn.
MRS PUTNAM	I knew it! Goody Osburn were midwife to me three times. I begged you, Thomas, did I not? I begged him

	not to call Osburn because I feared her. My babies always shrivelled in her hands!
HALE	Take courage, you must give us all their names. How can you bear to see this child suffering? Look at her, Tituba. *(He is indicating BETTY on the bed.)* Look at her God-given innocence; her soul is so tender; we must protect her, Tituba; the Devil is out and preying on her like a beast upon the flesh of the pure lamb. God will bless you for your help.

(ABIGAIL rises, staring as though inspired and cries out.)

ABIGAIL	I want to open myself!
	(They turn to her startled. She is enraptured, as though in a pearly light.)
	I want the light of God, I want the sweet love of Jesus! I danced for the Devil; I saw him; I wrote in his book; I go back to Jesus; I kiss His hand. I saw Sarah Good with the Devil! I saw Goody Osburn with the Devil! I saw Bridget Bishop with the Devil!
	(As she is speaking, BETTY is rising from the bed, a fever in her eyes, and picks up the chant.)
BETTY	*(staring too)* I saw George Jacobs with the Devil! I saw Goody Howe with the Devil!
PARRIS	She speaks! *(He rushes to embrace BETTY)* She speaks!
HALE	Glory to God! It is broken, they are free!
BETTY	*(calling out hysterically and with great relief)* I saw Martha Bellows with the Devil!
ABIGAIL	I saw Goody Sibber with the Devil! *(It is rising to a great glee.)*
PUTNAM	The marshal, I'll call the marshal!
	(PARRIS is shouting a prayer of thanksgiving.)
BETTY	I saw Alice Barrow with the Devil!
	(The curtain begins to fall.)
HALE	*(As Putnam goes out)* Let the marshal bring irons!
ABIGAIL	I saw Goody Hawkins with the Devil!
BETTY	I saw Goody Bibber with the Devil!
ABIGAIL	I saw Goody Booth with the Devil!
	(On their ecstatic cries the curtain falls.)

(Act 1)

Carson McCullers: *The Member of the Wedding* (1950)

McCullers' play can be considered alongside the work of Lillian Hellman and Tennessee Williams as a representation of life in the South with its racial prejudice and barriers. Frankie is a twelve-year-old girl with romantic notions about life which she feels are frustrated by her environment and her age. Berenice is the black servant of the household; Mr Addams, Frankie's father; T.T. and Honey, two black Americans, the latter being Berenice's nephew. The time setting is during the Second World War, when with the need for black labour in the factories of the Northern states, thousands of black Americans left the South and found a new economic status and freedom.

FRANKIE	*(looking in the mirror)* Don't you honestly think it's pretty? Give me your candy opinion.
BERENICE	I never knew anyone so unreasonable! You ask me my candy opinion, I give you my candy opinion. You ask me again, and I give it to you again. But what you want is not my honest opinion, but my good opinion of something I know is wrong.
FRANKIE	I only want to look pretty.
BERENICE	Pretty is as pretty does. Ain't that right, T.T.? You will look well enough for anybody's wedding. Excepting your own.
	(MR ADDAMS enters through the hall door.)
MR ADDAMS	Hello, everybody. *(to FRANKIE)* I don't want you roaming round the streets all morning and not coming home at dinner time. Looks like I'll have to tie you up in the back yard.
FRANKIE	I had business to attent to. Papa, look!
MR ADDAMS	What is it, Miss Pickle-priss?
FRANKIE	Sometimes I think you have turned stone blind. You never even noticed my new dress.
MR ADDAMS	I thought it was a show costume.
FRANKIE	Show costume! Papa, why is it you don't ever notice what I have on or pay any serious mind to me? You just walk around like a mule with blinders on, not seeing or caring.
MR ADDAMS	Never mind that now. *(to T.T. and HONEY)* I need some help down at my store. My porter failed me again. I wonder if you or Honey could help me next week.
T.T.	I will if I can, sir, Mr Addams. What days would be convenient for you, sir?
MR ADDAMS	Say Wednesday afternoon.

T.T.	Now, Mr Addams, that's one afternoon I promised to work for Mr Finny, sir. I can't promise anything, Mr Addams. But if Mr Finny changes his mind about needing me, I'll work for you, sir.
Mr Addams	How about you, Honey?
Honey	*(shortly)* I ain't got the time.
Mr Addams	I'll be so glad when the war is over and you biggety, worthless niggers get back to work. And furthermore, you *sir* me! Hear me!
Honey	*(reluctantly)* Yes – sir.
Mr Addams	I better go back to the store now and get my nose down to the grindstone. You stay home, Frankie. *(He goes out through the hall door.)*
John Henry	Uncle Royal called Honey a nigger. Is Honey a nigger?
Berenice	Be quiet now, John Henry. *(to Honey)* Honey, I got a good mind to shake you till you spit. Not saying sir to Mr Addams and acting so impudent.
Honey	T. T. said sir enough for a whole crowd of niggers. But for folks that calls me nigger, I got a real good nigger razor. *(He takes a razor from his pocket. FRANKIE and JOHN HENRY crowd close to look. When JOHN HENRY touches the razor, HONEY says)* Don't touch it, Butch, it's sharp. Liable to hurt yourself.
Berenice	Put up that razor, Satan! I worry myself sick over you. You going to die before your appointed span.
John Henry	Why is Honey a nigger?
Berenice	Jesus knows.
Honey	I'm so tensed up. My nerves been scraped with a razor. Berenice, loan me a dollar.
Berenice	I ain't handing you no dollar, worthless, to get high on them reefer cigarettes.
Honey	Gimme, Berenice, I'm so tensed up and miserable. The nigger hole. I'm sick of smothering in the nigger hole. I can't stand it no more.

(Relenting, Berenice gets her pocket-book from the shelf, opens it, and takes out some change.)

Berenice	Here's thirty cents. You can buy two beers.
Honey	Well, thankful for tiny, infinitesimal favors. I better be dancing off now.

(Act 2)

James Baldwin: *Blues for Mister Charlie* (1964)

Blues for Mister Charlie was one of the few plays written by a black American writer to penetrate the white-dominated cathedral of American theatre. It was produced at a time when the struggle for civil rights by black Americans was reaching its height and many blacks were beginning to think that peaceful protests were not bringing change quickly enough. Militant black groups, such as the organisation led by the later assassinated Malcolm X, were advocating armed struggle to bring about radical change in the attitudes of the white establishment. In this extract from the play, Meridian, a black preacher whose activist son has been killed by the local white police chief, argues with a sympathetic white newspaper editor about the appropriate strategy to deal with prejudice and violence against black Americans.

PARNELL   I hear it was real bad tonight.

MERIDIAN   Not as bad as it's going to get. Maybe I was wrong not to let the people arm.

PARNELL   If the Negroes were armed, it's the Negroes who'd be slaughtered. You know that.

MERIDIAN   They're slaughtered anyway. And I don't know that. I thought I knew it – but now I'm not so sure.

PARNELL   What's come over you? What's going to happen to the people in this town, this church – if you go to pieces?

MERIDIAN   Maybe they'll find a leader who can lead them some place.

PARNELL   Somebody with a gun? *(MERIDIAN is silent)* Is that what you mean?

MERIDIAN   I'm a Christian. I've been a Christian all my life, like my Mama and Daddy before me and like their Mama and Daddy before them. Of course, if you go back far enough, you get to a point *before* Christ, if you see what I mean, *B.C.* – and at that point, I've been thinking, black people weren't raised to turn the other cheek, and in the hope of heaven. No, then they didn't have to take low. Before Christ. They walked around as good as anybody else, and when they died, they didn't go to heaven, they went to join their ancestors. My son's dead, but he's not gone to join his ancestors. He was a sinner, so he must have gone to hell – if we're going to believe what the Bible says. Is that such an improvement, such a mighty advance over B.C. I've been thinking, I've had to think – would I have *been* such a Christian if I hadn't been born black? Maybe I *had* to become a Christian in order to have any dignity at all.

Since I wasn't a man in men's eyes, then I could be a man in the eyes of God. But that didn't protect my wife. She's dead, too soon, we don't really know how. That didn't protect my son – he's dead, we know how too well. That hasn't changed this town – this town where you couldn't find a white Christian at high noon on Sunday! The eyes of God – maybe those eyes are blind – I never let myself think of that before.

PARNELL   Meridian, you can't be the man who gives the signal for the holocaust.

MERIDIAN   Must I be the man who watches while his people are beaten, chained, starved, clubbed, butchered?

PARNELL   You used to say that your people were all the people in the world – all the people God ever made, or would make. You said your race was the human race.

MERIDIAN   The human race!

PARNELL   I've never seen you like this before. There's something in your tone I've never heard before – rage – maybe hatred –

MERIDIAN   You've heard it before. You just never recognised it before. You've heard it in all those blues and spirituals and gospel songs you claim to love so much.

PARNELL   I was talking about *you* – not your history. I have a history, too. And don't be so sure I've never heard that sound. Maybe I've never heard anything else. Perhaps my life is also hard to bear.

MERIDIAN   I watched you all this week up at the Police Chief's office with me. And you know how to handle him because you're sure you're better than he is. But you both have more in common with each other than either of you have with me. And, for both of you – I watched this, I never watched it before – it was just a black boy that was dead, and that was a problem. He saw the problem one way, you saw it another way. But it wasn't a *man* that was dead, not my *son* – you held yourselves away from *that*!

PARNELL   I may have sounded – cold. It was not because I felt cold. There was no other way to sound, Meridian. I took the only tone which – it seemed to me – could accomplish what we wanted. And I *do* know the Chief of Police better than you – because I'm white. And I can make him listen to me – because I'm white. I don't know that I think I'm so much better than he is. I know what we have done – and do. But you must have mercy on us. We have no other hope.

MERIDIAN	You have never shown us any mercy at all.
PARNELL	Meridian, give me credit for knowing you're in pain. We are two men, two friends – in spite of all that could divide us. We have come too far together, there is too much at stake, for you to become black now, for me to become white. Don't accuse me. Don't accuse me. *I* didn't do it.
MERIDIAN	So was my son – innocent.
PARNELL	Meridian – when I asked for mercy a moment ago – I meant – please – please try to understand that it is not easy to leap over fences, to give things up – all right, to surrender privilege! But if you were among the privileged you would know what I mean. It's not a matter of trying to hold *on*; the things, the privilege – are part of you, are *who* you are. It's in the gut.
MERIDIAN	Then where's the point of this struggle, where's the hope? If Mister Charlie can't change –
PARNELL	Who's Mister Charlie?
MERIDIAN	You're Mister Charlie. *All* white men are Mister Charlie!
PARNELL	You sound more and more like your son, do you know that? A lot of the coloured people here didn't approve of him, but he said things they longed to say – said right out loud, for all the world to hear, how much he despised white people!

(Act 1)

Edward Albee: *The American Dream* (1961)

In *The American Dream* Albee appears to be satirising American materialism, conformity and the ideal of conventional family life as an essential part of that dream. His early one-act play, *Zoo Story,* had been accepted as an example of the theatre of the absurd and there are certainly distinctively absurdist elements in *The American Dream*: characters are presented as symbols rather than as individuals; there is an absence of logical narrative in the play; the characters behave and speak oddly; the world is presented as a chaotic, arbitrary place where nothing much seems to make sense. Albee is presenting a parody of conventional American life. In this scene from the play, a Young Man, whom Grandma calls 'The American Dream', has wandered into the house on the off-chance that he might find some gainful employment. Grandma thinks he may be the 'van man' who Mommy and Daddy have arranged to take her to a home.

(The Young Man enters. Grandma looks him over.)

Young Man	Hello there.
Grandma	My, my, my. Are you the van man?
Young Man	The what?
Grandma	The van man. The van man. Are you come to take me away?
Young Man	I don't know what you're talking about.
Grandma	Oh. *(Pause)* Well. *(Pause)* My, my, aren't you something.
Young Man	Oh. Thank you.
Grandma	You don't sound very enthusiastic.
Young Man	Oh, I'm ... I'm used to it.
Grandma	Yup, yup. You know, if I were about a hundred and fifty years younger, I could go for you.
Young Man	Yes, I imagine so.
Grandma	Unh-hunh ... will you look at those muscles!
Young Man	*(flexing his muscles)* Yes, they're quite good, aren't they?
Grandma	Boy, they sure are. They natural?
Young Man	Well, the basic structure was there, but I've done some work too ... you know, in a gym.
Grandma	I'll bet you have. You ought to be in the movies, boy.
Young Man	I know.
Grandma	Yup! Right up there on the old silver screen. But I suppose you've heard that before.
Young Man	Yes, I have.
Grandma	You ought to try out for them ... the movies.
Young Man	Well, actually, I may have a career there yet. I've lived out on the West Coast almost all my life ... and I've met a few people who ... might be able to help me. I'm not in too much of a hurry, though. I'm almost as young as I look.
Grandma	Oh, that's nice. And will you look at that face!
Young Man	Yes, it's quite good, isn't it? Clean-cut, midwest farm boy type, almost insultingly good-looking in a typically American way. Good profile, straight nose, honest eyes, wonderful smile ...
Grandma	Yup. Boy, you know what you are, don't you? You're the American Dream, that's what you are. All those other people, they don't know what they're talking about. You ... *you* are the American Dream.
Young Man	Thanks.
Mommy	*(off stage)* Who rang the doorbell?

GRANDMA	(shouting off stage) The American Dream!
MOMMY	(off stage) What? What was that, Grandma?
GRANDMA	(shouting) The American Dream! The American Dream! Damn it!
DADDY	(off stage) How's that, Mommy?
MOMMY	(off stage) Oh, some gibberish. Pay no attention. Did you find Grandma's room?
DADDY	(off stage) No. I can't even find Mrs Barker.
YOUNG MAN	What was all that?
GRANDMA	That was just the folks, but let's not talk about them, honey; let's talk about you.
YOUNG MAN	All right.
GRANDMA	Well, let's see. If you're not the van man, what are you doing here?
YOUNG MAN	I'm looking for work.
GRANDMA	Are you? Well, what kind of work?
YOUNG MAN	Oh, almost anything ... almost anything that pays. I'll do almost anything for money.
GRANDMA	Will you ... will you? Hmmmmm. I wonder if there's anything you could do round here?
YOUNG MAN	There could be. It looked to be a likely building.
GRANDMA	It's always looked to be a rather unlikely building to me, but I suppose you know better than I.
YOUNG MAN	I can sense these things.
GRANDMA	There might be something you could do round here. Stay there! Don't come any closer.
YOUNG MAN	Sorry.
GRANDMA	I don't mean I'd mind. I don't know whether I'd mind or not ... But it wouldn't look well; it would look just awful.
YOUNG MAN	Yes, I suppose so.
GRANDMA	Now stay there, let me concentrate. What could you do? The folks have been in something of a quandary around here today, sort of a dilemma, and I wonder if you mightn't be of some help.
YOUNG MAN	I hope so ... if there's money in it.

Arthur Kopit: *Indians* (1968)

In *Indians* Kopit represents the heroic myths associated with the opening-out and settlement of the American West as bogus and dishonest. The mythology cannot disguise the harsh reality that something close to genocide was condoned in the wars against Native Americans who resisted the seizure of the lands they had inhabited for centuries. It is clear from the timing of the play that Kopit was not only commenting on American history in the latter part of the 19th century, but also intending his narrative to be a parable of what was happening in Vietnam in the 1960s. Kopit's use of American historical events to comment on contemporary political situations can be compared with Arthur Miller's employment of the Massachusetts witchcraft trials in *The Crucible* to comment on the McCarthyite persecutions of the 1950s. In this extract from the play, reporters are questioning the officer in charge of an attack on an Indian reservation which has resulted in the wholesale massacre of Native Americans.

FIRST REPORTER	Colonel Forsyth, some people are referring to your victory as a massacre. How do you feel about that?
COLONEL	One can always find someone who'll call an overwhelming victory a massacre. I suppose they'd prefer it if we'd let more of our own boys get shot!
FIRST REPORTER	Then you don't think the step you took was harsh?
COLONEL	Of course, it was harsh. And I don't like it any more than you. But had we shirked our responsibility, skirmishes would have gone on for years, costing our country millions, as well as untold lives. Of course, innocent people have been killed. In war they always are. And of course our hearts go out to the innocent victims of this. But war is not a game. It's tough. And demands tough decisions. In the long run I believe what happened here at this reservation yesterday will be justified.
FIRST REPORTER	Are you implying that the Indian Wars are finally over?
COLONEL	Yes, I believe they're finally over. The ludicrous buffalo religion of Sitting Bull's people was their last straw.
SECOND REPORTER	And now?
COLONEL	The difficult job of rehabilitation begins. But that's more up General Howard's line.
LIEUTENANT	Why don't we go and talk with him? He's in the temporary barracks.

COLONEL	He can tell you about our future plans. *(They start to leave.)*
BUFFALO BILL	You said you'd –
LIEUTENANT	Ah, yes, it's that one. *(He points to a body.)*
BUFFALO BILL	Thank you. *(He stays. The others leave; he stares at the grave. SITTING BULL has entered, unnoticed. BUFFALO BILL takes a sprig of pine from the satchel and is about to put it on the grave.)*
SITTING BULL	Wrong grave. I'm over here ... As you see, the dead can be buried, but not so easily gotten rid of.
BUFFALO BILL	Why didn't you listen to me? I *warned* you what would happen! Why didn't you *listen*? *(Long silence)*
SITTING BULL	We had land ... You wanted it, you took it. That ... I understand. What I cannot understand is why you did all this, *and at the same time* ... professed your love. *(Pause)*
BUFFALO BILL	Well ... well ... what about *your* mistakes? *Hm*? For, for example: you were very unrealistic ... about things. For ... example: did you *really* believe the buffalo would return? *Magically* return?
SITTING BULL	It seemed no less likely than Christ's returning, and a great deal more useful. Though when I think of their reception here, I can't see why either would really want to come back.
BUFFALO BILL	Oh, God. Imagine. For a while, I actually thought my Wild West Show would *help*. I could give you money. Food. Clothing. And also make people *understand* things ... better. *(He laughs to himself)* That was my reasoning. Or anyway, *part* ... *(Pause)* of my reasoning.
SITTING BULL	*(slight smile)* Your show was very popular. *(Pause)*
BUFFALO BILL	We had ... *fun* though, you and I. *(Pause)* Didn't we?
SITTING BULL	Oh, yes. And that's the terrible thing. We had all surrendered. We were on reservations. We could not fight, or hunt. We could do nothing. Then you came and allowed us to imitate our glory ... It was humiliating! For sometimes, we could almost imagine it was *real*.
BUFFALO BILL	Guess it wasn't so authentic, was it? *(He laughs slightly to himself.)*

Sitting Bull	How could it have been? You'd have killed all your performers in one afternoon. *(Pause)*
Buffalo Bill	You know what worried me most? … The fear that I might die, in the middle of the arena with all my … make-up on. *That* … is what … worried me most.
Sitting Bull	What worried *me* most was something I'd said the year before. Without thinking.
Buffalo Bill	*(Softly)* What?
Sitting Bull	I'd agreed to go onto the reservation. I was standing in front of my tribe, the soldiers leading us into the fort. And as we walked, I turned to my son, who was beside me. 'Now,' I said, 'you will never know what it is to be an Indian, for you will never have a gun or pony … .' Only later did I *realise* what I'd said. These things, the gun and the pony – they came with you. And then I thought, ah, how terrible it would be if we finally owe to the white man not only our destruction, but also our glory … Farewell, Cody. You were my friend. And, indeed, you still are. I never killed you … because I *knew it would not matter*. *(He starts to leave.)*
Buffalo Bill	If only I could have saved *your* life! *(Sitting Bull stops and stares at him coldly; turns and leaves.)*
	(Scene 13)

Sam Shepard: *Buried Child* (1979)

Many of Sam Shepard's plays seem to be concerned with the decay of the ideals associated with the opening-up of the American West by pioneers and small homesteaders. In Shepard's plays, he represents small ranchers being forced out of business by huge conglomerates, as fertile grazing land is given over to companies intent on oil exploration. Shepard is also interested in representing on stage what it means to be 'masculine' in an era where male roles seem to be changing and the old masculine ideal of 'manliness' more and more questioned. Another central feature of his work is the representation of dysfunctional family life. *Buried Child* encompasses all these themes. In this extract from the play, Tilden, who seems to be recovering from some kind of breakdown but is somehow associated with the land and farming, is confronted by his son Vince, whom he hasn't seen for years and whom he doesn't seem to recognise. Dodge is Tilden's drunken father; Shelly, Vince's friend; and Halie, who is mentioned, is the mother of the family who seems to have left home suddenly.

(Suddenly TILDEN *walks on from stage left just as he did before. This time his arms are full of carrots.* DODGE, VINCE *and* SHELLY *stop suddenly when they see him. They all stare at* TILDEN *as he crosses slowly center stage with the carrots and stops.* DODGE *sits on sofa, exhausted.)*

DODGE   *(panting, to* TILDEN*)* Where in the hell have you been?

TILDEN   Out back.

DODGE   Where's my bottle?

TILDEN   Gone.

*(*TILDEN *and* VINCE *stare at each other.* SHELLY *backs away.)*

DODGE   *(to* TILDEN*)* You stole my bottle!

VINCE   *(to* TILDEN*)* Dad?

*(*TILDEN *just stares at* VINCE*.)*

DODGE   You had no right to steal my bottle! No right at all!

VINCE   *(to* TILDEN*)* It's Vince. I'm Vince.

*(*TILDEN *stares at* VINCE *then looks at* DODGE *then turns to* SHELLY*.)*

TILDEN   *(after pause)* I picked these carrots. If anybody wants
             any carrots, I picked 'em.

SHELLY   *(to* VINCE*)* This is your father?

VINCE   *(to* TILDEN*)* Dad, what're you doing here?

*(*TILDEN *just stares at* VINCE, *holding carrots,* DODGE *pulls the blanket back over himself.)*

DODGE   *(to* TILDEN*)* You're going to have to get me another
             bottle! You gotta get me a bottle before Halie comes
             back! There's money on the table. *(Points to stage left
             kitchen.)*

TILDEN   *(shaking his head)* I'm not going down there.
             Into town.

*(*SHELLY *crosses to* TILDEN*.* TILDEN *stares at her.)*

SHELLY   *(to* TILDEN*)* Are you Vince's father?

TILDEN   *(to* SHELLY*)* Vince?

SHELLY   *(pointing to* VINCE*)* This is supposed to be your son! Is
             he your son? Do you recognise him? I'm just along for
             the ride here. I thought everybody knew each other!

*(*TILDEN *stares at* VINCE*.* DODGE *wraps himself up in the blanket and sits on sofa staring at the floor.)*

TILDEN   I had a son once but we buried him.

*(*DODGE *quickly looks at* TILDEN*.* SHELLY *looks to* VINCE*.)*

DODGE   You shut up about that! You don't know anything
             about that!

VINCE   Dad, I thought you were in New Mexico. We were going
             to drive down there to see you.

TILDEN   Long way to drive.

DODGE	*(to TILDEN)* You don't know anything about that! That happened before you were born! Long before!
VINCE	What's happened, Dad? What's going on here? I thought everything was all right. What's happened to Halie?
TILDEN	She left.
SHELLY	*(to TILDEN)* Do you want me to take those carrots for you?

(TILDEN stares at her. She moves in close to him. Holds out her arms. TILDEN stares at her arms then slowly dumps the carrots into her arms. SHELLY stands there holding the carrots.)

TILDEN	*(to SHELLY)* You like carrots?
SHELLY	Sure. I like all kinds of vegetables.
DODGE	*(to TILDEN)* You gotta get me a bottle before Halie comes back! *(DODGE hits sofa with his fist. VINCE crosses up to DODGE and tries to console him. SHELLY and TILDEN stay facing each other.)*
TILDEN	*(to SHELLY)* Back yard's full of carrots. Corn. Potatoes.
SHELLY	You're Vince's father, right?
TILDEN	All kinds of vegetables. You like vegetables?
SHELLY	*(laughs)* Yeah. I love vegetables.
TILDEN	We could cook these carrots, ya' know. You could cut 'em up and we could cook 'em.
SHELLY	All right.

(Act 2)

David Mamet: *American Buffalo* (1986)

Mamet's usual dramatic territory is that of small-time crime or con men of some kind, but the sub-text of his plays hints that his real target is American business methods, with what he sees as its get-rich-quick ethics and shady dealings. The street language of his 'characters' often echoes the rhetoric employed by American big business. Very often in Mamet's plays it is not what the characters say that is important but what is not being said. This extract from *American Buffalo* provides an example of this kind of sub-text. Don and Teach are planning a robbery of a valuable coin collection. The real subject of their discussion, however, may be Teach's quest for reassurance that Don rates him and values him as a friend and a fellow professional.

DON	I'm going to have Fletch come with us.
TEACH	Fletch.
DON	Yes.
TEACH	You're having him come with us.

Don	Yes.
Teach	Now you're kidding me.
Don	No.
Teach	No? Then why do you say this?
Don	With Fletch.
Teach	Yes.
Don	I want some depth.
Teach	You want depth on the team.
Don	Yes, I do.
Teach	So you bring in Fletch.
Don	Yes.
Teach	'Cause I don't play your games with you.
Don	We might just need him.
Teach	We won't.
Don	We might, Teach.
Teach	We don't need him, Don. We do not need this guy.

(DON *picks up phone.*)

Teach: What? Are you calling him?

(DON *nods.*)

Don	It's busy. (*Hangs up.*)
Teach	He's probably talking on the phone.
Don	Yeah. He probably is.
Teach	We don't need this guy, Don. We don't need him. I see your point here, I do. So you're thinking I'm out there alone, and you're worried I'll rattle, so you ask me how I go in. I understand. I see this, I do. I could go in the second floor, climb up a drainpipe, I could this ...

(DON *dials phone again.*)

Teach: He's talking, he's talking, for chrissake, give him a minute, huh?

(DON *hangs up phone.*)

Don	I'm sorry, Teach.
Teach	I'm not hurt for me.
Don	Who are you hurt for?
Teach	Think about it.
Don	We can use somebody watch our rear.
Teach	You keep your numbers down, you don't have a rear. You know what has rears? Armies.
Don	I'm just saying, something goes wrong ...
Teach	Wrong, wrong, you make your own right and wrong. Hey Biiig fucking deal. The shot is yours, no one's disputing that. We're talking business, let's talk business: you think it's a good business call Fletch in? To help us.

DON	Yes.
TEACH	Well then okay.
	(Pause)
	Are you sure?
DON	Yeah.
TEACH	All right, if you're sure …
DON	I'm sure, Teach.
TEACH	Then all right, then. That's all I worry about.
	(Pause)
	And you're probably right, we could use three of us on the job.
DON	Yeah.
TEACH	Somebody watch for the cops … work out a signal …
DON	Yeah.
TEACH	Safety in numbers.
DON	Yeah.
TEACH	Three-men jobs.
DON	Yeah.
TEACH	You, me, Fletcher.
DON	Yeah.
TEACH	A division of labor.
	(Pause)
	Security. Muscle. Intelligence. Huh?
DON	Yeah.
TEACH	This means, what, a traditional split. Am I right? We get ten off the top goes to Earl, and the rest, three-way split. Huh? That's what we got? Huh?
DON	Yeah.
TEACH	Well, that's what's right.
	(Pause)
	All right. Lay the shot out for me.

(Act 1)

4 | Critical approaches to 20th century American drama

Part 4 looks at the response of critics to the plays written by 20th century American playwrights.

- How far should the plays be viewed within the historical, social and cultural context in which they were written?

- What do the critics perceive to be the main strengths and weaknesses of the plays of major American dramatists?

- How do questions of gender and race influence our reading/critical opinion of the plays, given that the majority are written from a white, male perspective?

Some of the critics who are quoted here are professional critics who earn, or have earned, their living by writing reviews of theatrical productions, others are writers on cultural theory and trends, while still others concentrate on analysing social and political issues in American society and how these influence works of art such as plays. The quotations from these critics are intended to set you thinking about specific plays and dramatists and to encourage you to perceive dramatic works within their specific historical, social and cultural context. The opinions are there for you to agree with or to disagree with.

1915–41: the plays of O'Neill, Odets and others

Eugene O'Neill

Almost all critics are agreed that it is with the production of Eugene O'Neill's early plays that American drama found its first authentic voice. Yet O'Neill was writing about a society he felt increasingly alienated from. Alan Trachtenberg is a contemporary American critic interested in viewing plays within their social and cultural context. Trachtenberg summarised the dilemma facing O'Neill and other writers in these words: 'What place for the serious artist in a society without active standards of decency, decorum and moral intelligence?' Trachtenberg describes the development of American society in the early decades of the century thus: 'a pattern of steady accumulation of wealth, of population, of industrial power, of rationalisation of production and business organisation, the emergence of a nationwide transport-communications system for rapid distribution of goods and the consumer values and ideals accompanying them, and also of visible difference in the distribution of wealth, power and abundance'.

Trachtenberg in the same essay identifies the influence of psychoanalytical theory on writers, as well the cultural influence of modernism from Europe: 'By the 1920s Freudianism had joined modernism in questioning the autonomy of will and conscious choice; like modern art, it evoked images of dark subterranean forces.' Lillian Feder, an American academic writing from the perspective of the 1980s, writes of O'Neill: 'In writing modern tragedy, O'Neill enlarged Strindberg's view of irresolvable human conflict through the Freudian tragic conception of illumination as both the price and the reward of acknowledging unconscious drives … His last and greatest plays, *Long Day's Journey into Night* … and *The Iceman Cometh* … reveal a deeper insight into the unconscious processes that determine human behaviour.' Christopher Bigsby, a contemporary British critic and writer on American drama of the 20th century, notes that for O'Neill 'theatre was trivial if it did not tackle what he considered to be the "big issues"'.

Warren French, in a book that deals with American literature of the 20th century as a whole, emphasises the influence of cultural movements on O'Neill: 'all his plays are modernist statements of the need of individuals to escape the deadly restraints of monotonous lives or oppressive institutions'. To Christopher Bigsby, *The Emperor Jones* is 'on one level … a comment on imperialism, as it is an assault on the more obvious presumptions of racism'.

Jean Chothia is a contemporary writer who has written about O'Neill's forging of a specific American language in his plays. In an essay 'Eugene O'Neill and real realism', Chothia writes that the 'late plays' *Long Day's Journey* and *Iceman* 'draw more directly on O'Neill's personal life than anything he had previously written but, wholly dramatic, flexible in their dialogue, fully achieved in their form, they succeed in moving beyond the private to convey the essence of American – indeed, Western – experience in our time: the restlessness of the mobile society, the tensions within the nuclear family, the isolation and inarticulacy of the individual, the way in which the past shapes and haunts the present'. However, Bigsby alerts us to what he sees as weaknesses in O'Neill's drama: 'Even *The Iceman Cometh* … presses character and image too far, surrendering to its own logic.'

► Read O'Neill's play *The Iceman Cometh* and consider Bigsby's comment above that O'Neill 'presses character and image too far, surrendering to its own logic', meaning that the characters behave like puppets manoeuvred by the dramatist to react to dramatic events in predetermined ways. From your reading of the play, how accurate do you think Bigsby's comment is?

Elmer Rice

Not all critics accept that drama need be viewed within its social and historical context. John Gassner, an American critic writing almost fifty years ago, states: 'It cannot be stressed too greatly that the playwrights of the twenties painted a picture not to be taken at face value ... There is an art to understanding art that neither sociologists nor politicians seem to have quite mastered.' Writing about Elmer Rice's 1929 naturalistic drama *Street Scene*, Gassner says, 'Dramatic treatments of such themes in the thirties would have ended in a conversion to radicalism as in Odets' *Awake and Sing!*. But the dramatist of the twenties ... was apt to take the facts and let the moral go. Salvation was ... a theatrical discovery of the depression decade in America.'

Over twenty years later, Bernard Dukore, however, in writing about the same Rice play takes a totally different standpoint: 'Many of these characters are shaped by the same socio-economic environment as the ciphers of *The Adding Machine*. They cannot think for themselves, but repeat empty slogans and attitudes created by non-education, mal-education, and newspapers that catering to the lowest common denominator mould ideas.' Criticism over the last twenty years has become much more aware of the need to evaluate works of drama and literature within a specific social and historical context. The quotes from Gassner and Dukore with their differing emphases illustrate this development in critical approaches. French sees *The Adding Machine* as 'a devastating picture of dehumanisation'. Bigsby also pairs Rice with Odets: 'Like Odets, Rice was concerned in *Street Scene* with the hyphenated Americans in their struggle to discover the essence of the world to which they wish to assimilate themselves.'

Maxwell Anderson

Writing about the plays of Maxwell Anderson, Bernard Dukore – again emphasising the need to identify themes that mirror social and political trends in the society of the time – comments: 'Woven throughout his variegated drama are views of individualism; social institutions that thwart, oppress and plunder individuals; rebels who defy society; and questions of integrity.' At the same time as considering Anderson a serious dramatist, Dukore describes his attempts at dramatic verse as 'windy and poor'. About Anderson's play *Winterset,* Bigsby writes 'his subject was less the hysterical politics of his own period than the fact of injustice and the eternal struggle to oppose it'. However, a contemporary reviewer of the play, John Mason Brown, emphasises what he identifies as an artistic weakness and describes Anderson's verse as an attempt at dressing up 'some very indifferent generalities in some extremely gaudy plumage'.

▶ Read the extract from Elmer Rice's play *The Adding Machine* on pages 61–63. One of the critics quoted above describes the play as 'a devastating picture of dehumanisation'. Does this extract from the play bear out what this critic says?

▶ Read the extract from Maxwell Anderson's play *Winterset* on pages 65–67. A critic quoted above describes the verse of the play as 'windy and poor'. Do you think this is a fair assessment? What is your response to Anderson's attempt to use dramatic verse?

Clifford Odets

On Clifford Odets, Dukore has this to say: 'Perhaps Odets' most notable quality is language. His characters' speech combines American wisecracks, period slang, Jewish-American speech of the time and intrinsically apt imagery.' French writes of Odets' *Awake and Sing!* as 'Odets' most enduring work' and describes it as '*the* American depression play, a still vital example of the 1930s conviction that, however terrible the situation, it could be rectified by an infusion of idealistic rhetoric administered at the final curtain'. He also sees the play as a product not only of Odets' talent but of the theatrical context in which it was written: 'Odets was a member of the Group Theatre, an acting company that was a family of sorts, and his Bergers are an echo of the loving, quarrelling Group company which was a home for Odets.'

For Bigsby, Odets in *Awake and Sing!* is 'less interested in offering an indictment of capitalism than he is with asserting the need for a morally improved world, for the individual to wake up to a failure which is as much private as public'. The mood of the play, for this critic, 'is much closer to Roosevelt than Marx'. By this he means that the political message is closer to the reformist policies of President Roosevelt, who was elected to power in 1932 on the promise of delivering 'New Deal' policies and reforming the less acceptable aspects of capitalism (see page 12) than the communist economics of Karl Marx, the philosopher who preached that only the overthrow of the capitalist system could cure the injustices of capitalist society.

▶ A critic quoted above says Clifford Odets' 'most notable quality is language – American wisecracks, period slang'. Read the extract from *Waiting for Lefty* on pages 67–70 and comment on Odets' use of language in the light of this comment.

Lillian Hellman

Brooks Atkinson, an American theatre critic who wrote his reviews of plays and critical works during the period when these plays were first produced on the stage, identifies Lillian Hellman as 'the representative of the well-made play'. Dukore agrees and says that her plays are also 'parables, sometimes obvious, sometimes not'. But he finds her wanting in some aspects of her writing: 'Unlike Ibsen's, her issues are cut-and-dried and her discussions confirm, not challenge, our judgements.' He analyses the social and historical significance of *The Little Foxes* in this way: 'It requires little imagination to recognise in the foxes the fascists who had begun to devour the earth, in the defeated Birdie decayed European aristocracy, in the dying father Horace European capitalism too weak to intervene effectively and in young Alexandra hope that America would fight.' For Bigsby, the play is 'recognisably American' and 'Southern' with a 'constant intersection of past and present, myth and history, social custom and sexual behaviour'.

William Saroyan

Howard R. Floan, writing in 1966 about a play first staged in 1939, views Saroyan's play *The Time of Your Life* as being 'about a state of mind, illusive but real, whose readily recognisable components are, first, an awareness of America's youth – its undisciplined swaggering, unregulated early life – and secondly, a pervasive sense of America in crisis: an America of big business, of labour strife, of depersonalised government and, above all, of imminent war'. Dukore also recognises the centrality of Saroyan's vision of America: 'Saroyan's temperament is that of the freewheeling Californian individualist, an American writ large. To Saroyan grime hides purity, love is beautiful and universal, life can, if you permit it, be mellow or exuberant.' Of the dramatic elements that make up the play, a contemporary review noted that it was 'a sort of cosmic vaudeville show, formless, plotless and shamelessly rambling, it is a helter-skelter mixture of humour, sentimentalism, philosophy and melodrama, and one of the most enchanting works imaginable'.

Thornton Wilder

Dukore notes that Thornton Wilder's plays 'suggest archetypal America, which he celebrates as warm, innocent, religious, simple and simply nice. His theatrical forms are in the vanguard of modernism. But his themes are not modernist: he does not urge social activism, convey despair at the human condition or stress sexuality.' Brooks Atkinson sees *Our Town* and its representation of Grover's Corners as 'a living fragment of the universe, indigenous not merely to New Hampshire, but to the life of man'. For Bigsby, *Our Town* is an example of Wilder 'the poet at work'. Wilder is aiming at 'a sense of life as ritual, and an attempt to insist on a spiritual continuity'.

Dukore sums up the achievement of the American dramatists of the 1920s and 1930s in this way: 'At their best these works have distinctly American vitality and affirmation, as if the first wave of important American dramatists were proclaiming to the Old World the buoyant energies of the New and its faith in the future, however precarious the present seemed.'

1941–60: the plays of Miller, Williams and others

Arthur Miller

For Christopher Bigsby, Miller 'time after time ... explores the lives of those who fail to acknowledge their freedom to act'. For Bigsby, 'human fallibility' is Miller's central subject: 'The problem was never capitalism or coercive conformity, anti-semitism or totalitarianism, but the very human nature which in other respects is the only possible defence against those reductive forces.' Brenda Murphy, in an essay linking Miller with Ibsen and other 'social drama' playwrights, stresses that 'Miller was trying to define a tradition that would encompass both the psycho-logical and the social' and that 'the concept of the "whole" man – psyche and citizen, individual subject and social actor – has driven Miller's own play writing from very early on'.

To Matthew C. Roudané, a contemporary critic, *Death of a Salesman* 'presents a rich matrix of enabling fables that define the myth of the American Dream'. Willy Loman, Miller's 'common man' hero, values principles such as 'initiative, hard work, family, freedom, consumerism, economic salvation, competition, the frontier, self-sufficiency, public recognition, personal fulfilment' that comprise that American Dream. Feminist critics, Roudané notes, however, have criticised *Salesman* for apparently making the concerns of women peripheral and viewed only from a male perspective. Linda Kintz, for example, sees the play as offering 'a nostalgic view of the plot of the universalised masculine protagonist'. However, Bigsby states that Miller saw Loman as a 'representative figure because he carried in his pocket 'the courage of our day'. Bigsby here directly links the play to specific political events of the 1930s, clearly identifying it as an artistic product of its time.

Lillian Feder analyses Miller's use of expressionist sets, music and imaginary conversations through which he 'conveys the breakdown of the psychic defences that have formed the symbolic salesman's version of the American dream of success'. However, for Feder, Willy 'remains rooted in his time and place, a moving domestic figure who is never quite at home in the expressionist structure meant to enlarge him'. Feder asserts that Miller fails to create modern tragic drama not only in *Salesman* but also in *The Crucible* and *A View from the Bridge* because 'their action depends too heavily on the limitations of a single character intended as representative, but too naturalistically drawn to assume that stature'.

Indeed, Stephen Barker, another contemporary critic, has written that 'Miller's critical reception, particularly in his native America, has been mixed, at times downright hostile'. Bigsby offers a partial explanation for this: 'America finally does not want to be told that innocence can ever be lost, that a condition of after the fall exists and so cannot accept Miller's world-view; in America Miller's vision is thus incompatible with the individualistic (yet mass-oriented) American dream.'

Tennessee Williams

Roudáne emphasises Tennessee Williams' celebration of language: 'He sought to find the verbal equivalents for his characters' tortured selves, a search that led him away from the realism of Ibsen, O'Casey, (the later) O'Neill, Clifford Odets and Lillian Hellman and towards a new dramatic form.' Discussing Williams' 'plastic theatre', Roudáne claims that Williams created 'a lyric drama, a poetic theatre'. 'Plastic theatre' is Williams' term for a symbolic, non-realist, metaphorical theatre which uses objects, musical underscoring, costumes, props and theatrical space to create an experience for the audience that suggests poetic truths.

Bigsby links two of Miller's plays and two of Williams' in this way: '*Death of a Salesman* and *The Crucible*, *The Glass Menagerie* and *A Streetcar Named Desire* seemed to suggest the end of a particular model of America and of individual character ... Basic Myths having to do with family and community, civility and responsibility, style and grace had dissolved. The future seemed to offer little more than a bland materialism or a drugged conformity.' Bigsby sees Laura Wingfield in Williams' play *The Glass Menagerie* 'as a paradigm of the culture of which she is a part. The world of modernity, the dance hall and the typewriter, is outside of her experience. Vulnerable, she chooses instead a world of myth, symbolised by the glass unicorn.' Blanche Dubois in *A Streetcar Named Desire* also inhabits, for Bigsby, a world of myth: 'Blanche enters the play, an actress creating her own entrance ... Whatever was natural, whatever was spontaneous, whatever was true seems to have given way to performance.'

For Felicia Londré, in an essay on *A Streetcar Named Desire*, the play encompasses everything that is characteristic of Williams' drama: 'the episodic structure, the lyricism of dialogue and atmosphere interspersed by comedy; the psychological realism of the characterisations set against striking departures from realism in the staging; the evocatively charged use of scenic elements, props, sound effects, gestures, and linguistic motifs; and the focus on characters who are psychically wounded or otherwise marginalised by mainstream society: characters seeking lost purity, or escape from the ravages of time, or refuge from the harshness of an uncomprehending world, or simple human contact'.

Christopher Bigsby notes the social, and Southern, dimension of Williams' *Cat on a Hot Tin Roo*f: 'The disease from which Big Daddy suffers is uremia, defined as a "poisoning of the whole system due to the failure of the body to eliminate poisons". The disease from which his society suffers is essentially the same. Its governing principles are greed and mendacity, and Brick, in common with Laura in *The Glass Menagerie,* is ill-equipped to survive. As she is drawn to the child-like mythic world of her glass animals, he is attracted to the unproblematic mythic world of his former sporting successes on the football field and the track.' Bigsby also reminds us that Williams can be perceived as a 'Southern playwright' when he discusses his play *Sweet Bird of Youth,* which he sees as 'another indictment of Southern bigotry, another portrait of a terminal society trapped in its own myths'.

▶ Writing about the character of Blanche in Williams' *A Streetcar Named Desire* Bigsby states, '...whatever was true seems to have given way to performance'. Read the extract from *A Streetcar Named Desire* on pages 76–78 and analyse how relevant this idea of Blanche acting a part or giving a performance is to her actions and words in this section of the play.

William Inge

Writing of William Inge's play Come *Back Little Sheba*, John Gassner likens it to *The Glass Menagerie* in its 'concern with small lives and a sparing expenditure of plot'. Yet Gassner seems to imply a criticism of Williams' poetic or plastic theatre when he adds, 'unlike Tennessee Williams, Mr Inge resolutely allowed the facts of a constricted, essentially small-town life to speak for themselves, without the accessory machinery of narrations, flashbacks and symbolism'. For Bigsby, too, Inge's plays are about the smothering effect of small-town life: 'On the surface they had a gentle humour as innocents struggled with emotions new to them and tried to match ambitions and hopes to the diminished world of possibility.'

Lorraine Hansberry

Bigsby, writing about Lorraine Hansberry's *A Raisin' in the Sun,* explains that it is 'rooted in personal experience, an experience which turned on Hansberry's racial identity, and through the struggle of the Younger family for a sense of dignity, for a space within which self-definition can become possible, was not restricted to race'. He also notes that the play is ambivalent in its attitude to a white liberalism that expressed its support for the struggle of black Americans for equality but was limited in how far it would go to bring that equality about.

1960–90: the plays of Albee, Shepard, Mamet and others

Edward Albee, Sam Shepard and David Mamet are, for many critics, the three outstanding dramatists to emerge in this period. As these playwrights are still alive and writing new plays, critical comments on their work are by contemporary critics who do not have the same kind of historical perspective on their plays as they would have if they were writing about, say, the plays of Eugene O'Neill or Lillian Hellman. Fifty years from now, critics writing about Albee, Shepard and Mamet will doubtless view them from a different perspective.

Edward Albee

For critic Christopher Bigsby, Albee's 'fundamental theme' is 'the collapse of communality, the Other as threat. The overwhelming mood is elegiac. His subject is loss, desolation, spiritual depletion. But where in Beckett's work that would breed irony, here, at least in the early plays, it generates a faith in the possibility of redemption.' These early Albee plays, for Bigsby, call 'for a renewal of the spirit and the revival of liberal values. In that sense he was a product of the Kennedy years.' In this insight, Bigsby directly tries to relate the play to its specific historical context.

Critical opinions differ how on how much Albee's plays owe to the theatre of the absurd. For Martin Esslin, a contemporary writer who has written a great deal about world drama, Albee's play *Zoo Story* comes into the category of the theatre of the absurd precisely 'because his work attacks the very foundations of American optimism'. But Ronald Hayman contradicts that and questions whether the theatre of the absurd is 'a valid category' at all. Whereas Esslin attacks the violent ending of *Zoo Story* as melodramatic and sentimental, Hayman defends it in these words: 'Without killing his hero, Albee would not have been able to make the point that Jerry could not have got through to Peter in any other way, and the important question is not whether the action at the end looks melodramatic ... but whether the dialogue that leads up to it has successfully established the encounter between two strangers on a park bench as a valid analogue of human relationships in contemporary society and whether Peter is acceptable as a personification of contemporary conformism.'

For Peter Davison, Albee's 'prime dramatic strength' lies in 'his marvellous ear for certain kinds of dialogue – for empty chit-chat, lacerating sarcasm, and banality concealing hollow emotions – which he uses to serve his dramatic needs'. Albee's second strength, according to the same critic, 'is his fierce, even demonic, urge to expose what he takes to be the falseness of the American Dream'. The language of Albee's play of that title is analysed by Bigsby thus: 'The language of Mommy and Daddy in *The American Dream*, like the functional claims of their names, denied in action, is evacuated of meaning, conventionalised to the point that it becomes self-annihilating.' For Bigsby, Albee's plays are 'conversation pieces' and his subject 'the substitution of language for experience ... is equally his theatrical method'.

Bigsby reminds us that Albee himself explains the tone and mood of *Who's Afraid of Virginia Woolf?* 'as a product of the early 1960s, the Kennedy years'. For Davison, this play 'dramatises with raw ferocity what the American – or any other – Dream can be when superficial values have replaced true virtues'. For Ronald Hayman, however, *Virginia Woolf* is not 'a defeatist play' ... 'Basically, like *Zoo Story*, it is a play about making contact and here George and Martha have had a real contact with each other and with external reality.'

Sam Shepard

For critic Richard Gilman, 'the network of influences, interests and obsessions' that have helped to shape Sam Shepard's play are: 'the car or road culture of his youth, science-fiction, Hollywood Westerns and the myth of the West in general, and television in its pop or junk aspects'. Shepard's plays, Gilman writes, contain a 'rejection of linear construction, cause and effect sequences, logical procedures, coherent or consistent characters, and the tying of language to explicit meanings'. Bigsby, too, recognises a familiar 'American world' in Shepard's dramas: 'popular folklore, the familiar stereotype, the cartoon, the bric-a-brac of modern living, the theatrical properties of American experience'. Indeed, for Bigsby, Shepard was the first playwright 'to construct his drama out of the materials of the popular arts, to infiltrate the sounds and image of popular culture into work which rendered up its meaning less to those who approached it with an analytic mind than to those who chose to inhabit its images and respond to its rhythms on an emotional or visceral level'. For Gilman what is remarkable about Shepard's plays 'is the way they display the new raw unstable anguish and the wit that marks the self seeking itself now'.

David Mamet

To John Lahr, David Mamet belongs 'in the pantheon of this century's great dramatists'; his plays 'though rooted in reality, are fables, whose uniqueness lies in their distinctive music – a terse, streamlined orchestration of thought, language and character which draws viewers in and makes them work for meaning'. Lahr identifies the main themes of Mamet's work as 'the sense of not belonging, the imperative of speaking out, the betrayal of authority'. To Bigsby, Mamet 'explores the myths of capitalism, the loss of that spiritual confidence which was once presumed to underpin individual identity and national enterprise alike. The language of liberal concern and humane principle echoes through plays in which rhetoric seldom if ever matches the reality of character or action. Nor are rapacity and greed presented as the decadent products of history. In America, he implies, they were its motor force.' For this critic, Mamet 'combines a concern with the underside of the American Dream with a powerful social vision and a brilliant linguistic sensitivity to create plays of genuine originality'.

▶ One critic quoted above talks about Mamet's 'brilliant linguistic sensitivity'. Read the extract from *American Buffalo* on pages 95–97 and analyse how Mamet subtly suggests through the words his two characters speak what their real concerns are beneath the surface meaning of what they say.

Gender, racial and class perspectives

American theatre has been largely male-dominated. Writers such as Lillian Hellman, Carson McCullers and Lorraine Hansberry have made important contributions to American theatre, but, by and large, the American stage has presented plays by male writers, which reflects the fact that most producers and entrepreneurs working in the American theatre have been male. More female dramatists are now having their plays performed, partly because of the realisation that women writers have been under-represented, but also because producers have realised that plays written by women can find a wide audience and produce profits.

The reality of this 'gender bias', however, has important implications for the perspective from which we view these plays. Feminist critics believe that many male writers represent a male world in which female characters and concerns are either sidelined or distorted. Whether this is an accurate assessment or not, it is a perspective you should be aware of. For example, how does this 'male perspective' affect how we read the plays of David Mamet?

If American theatre has been dominated by male writers, it can also be stated that most successful American playwrights have been white Americans, albeit from different ethnic origins. Arthur Miller and Clifford Odets, for example, have immigrant Jewish roots, while Eugene O'Neill came from Irish stock. There have been many black American dramatists who have had their plays performed profess-ionally, but comparatively few have achieved success on Broadway or even in off-Broadway theatres and this can be nothing to do with a lack of innate talent. For whatever reason, it would appear that a racial bias is a factor in American theatre.

The vast majority of Broadway theatregoers are white, middle-class Americans with the result that commercial managements cater to what they perceive as the tastes of their target audience. Thus, another important perspective to bear in mind is race. For example, how accurate and meaningful would Tennessee Williams' representation of the American South in his plays be to a black American with a different experience of life in the South from a white American? Black Americans as characters are very thin on the ground in the plays of most important American dramatists, even in those written by radical playwrights such as Clifford Odets. How does this 'absence' affect how we interpret these plays? Is a play as much about what is not represented or 'said' as it is about what is represented and uttered? When a white American playwright such as Eugene O'Neill does represent blacks in his plays, as he does in *The Emperor Jones* and *All God's Chillun Got Wings*, should our reading of the play be shaped by the perspective that this is a white dramatist writing about the 'black experience'?

Bibliography of critical opinions

This list relates to the critical opinions quoted in this section.

Alan Trachtenberg 'The Social and Cultural Context in American Literature': Volume 9 of *The New Pelican Guide to English Literature*, edited by Boris Ford (Penguin, 1991)

Lilian Feder 'The Literary Scene' (source as above)

Peter Davison 'Tennessee Williams, Arthur Miller and Edward Albee' (source as above)

Jean Chothia 'Eugene O'Neill and Real Realism' (source as above)

Brooks Atkinson *Introduction to the Famous American Plays* (Random House, 1941)

Christopher Bigsby *A Critical Introduction to Twentieth Century American Drama* (Cambridge University Press, 1985)

Christopher Bigsby *Modern American Drama* 1945–90 (Cambridge University Press, 1992)

Bernard Dukore *American Dramatists* 1918–45 (Macmillan, 1984)

Warren French *Introduction to the 20th Century American Literature* (St Martin's Press, New York, 1980)

John Gassner *Introduction to Best American Plays* 1918–58 (Crown Publishers, New York, 1961)

Brenda Murphy 'The tradition of social drama: Miller and his forebears' in *The Cambridge Companion to Arthur Miller*, edited by Christopher Bigsby (Cambridge University Press, 1977)

Matthew C. Roudáne '*Death of a Salesman* and the poetics of Arthur Miller' (source as above)

Stephen Barker 'Critic, criticism, critics' (source as above)

Felicia Londré 'A streetcar running fifty years' in *The Cambridge Companion to Tennessee Williams*, edited by Matthew Roudáne (Cambridge University Press, 1997)

Richard Gilman *Introduction to Seven Plays: Sam Shepard* (Faber and Faber, 1981)

John Lahr 'Fortress Mamet', *New Yorker*, 17 November, 1997

5 | How to write about 20th century American drama

In Part 5, guidance is given about how to approach writing on 20th century American drama, including:

- the terminology

- the discussion of dramatic themes and subject matter

- the analysis of characterisation

- the use of quotations and close references to drama text

- how to use critical sources

- how to place plays within their social, cultural and historical context.

Writing about theme

It is perfectly relevant to discuss the thematic content of a play, as you interpret it, but always try to link your analysis to the text. For example, consider this example of thematic analysis of Tennessee Williams' play *A Streetcar Named Desire*:

> One of the recurring themes in Williams' plays is the fear of isolation and social ostracism. Blanche in *Streetcar* talks about having always had to depend on 'the kindness of strangers'. Any actress playing Blanche Dubois and saying this line would need to bring out that quality of vulnerability and pathos with which Williams has imbued the speech and the role.

Notice how this analysis moves from the general to the particular: the general point about a recurring theme in Williams' work is made and then backed up by a particular reference to a line in one of Williams' plays. In addition, there is the reminder that it is a *play* that is being discussed, a piece of drama that is open to interpretation in actual performance, by the actors and the director, and also by the audience.

Writing about the 'characters'

In the section on David Mamet on pages 46–48, the playwright is quoted as saying there are no characters in his plays, there are only lines on a page. In essence, this is true, because the 'characters' in any play are the product of a fusion of speech and dramatic action, created through the language chosen by the playwright and, indeed, in performance 'fleshed out' by an actor on stage. The characters of a play are not real human beings and do not actually exist beyond the page or the performance. They are creations, 'constructs' within a piece of drama.

Try in your writing to interpret how a 'character' is being used in a play, what the dramatist is trying to represent through any particular dramatic figure and what function in the drama as a whole 'he' or 'she' plays. Consider these two contrasting discussions of Hickey in Eugene O'Neill's play *The Iceman Cometh*:

1   Hickey is a sad man, who needs to persuade the customers of the bar that they all live according to illusionary pipe dreams. He wants them to face up to these illusions and to face up to life without that protection.

2   In Hickey, O'Neill has created a dramatic figure that represents the desperation that can ensue when an individual divests himself of the illusions that have protected him from the realities of his own unhappiness, and who now wants to spread the gospel among the walking wounded of the waterfront bar of the advantages of living life without this protection of 'pipe dreams'.

In 1, Hickey is discussed as though he were a real living being; in 2, the reference to the playwright and Hickey as a 'dramatic figure' within the play reminds us that he is a creation with a particular function within the text of the play. This is an important distinction and one you should pay attention to. The second analysis shows an awareness of how a play, and a character within the play, are constructed by a dramatist through language.

Drama in historical, social and cultural context

There has been an emphasis in this book on placing American drama of the 20th century within its historical, social and cultural context. That is, plays are to be perceived not just as the product of one dramatist's imagination, but as a reflection and, in part, a product, of their time. As well as the historical events of any given period that may be a shaping factor in how plays are created, there are also the cultural conditions and trends that may affect how plays are written. For example, in the 1920s playwrights such as Eugene O'Neill and Elmer Rice were undoubtedly influenced by expressionism, a trend in the arts in general which encouraged non-representational approaches. In the theatre, expressionism produced new dramatic forms that did not rely on logical plots, 'character' or realistic speech, but emphasised expressionist sets, imaginative lighting, unusual use of sound and speech and many other aspects of 'theatricality'. When you use terms such as 'expressionism', 'realism', 'social drama' or 'naturalism', do not use them without illustrating in specific terms how they are relevant to the play(s) under discussion.

Clearly, it is important not to overstate the direct link between a play text and the historical and social circumstances in which it was created. However, plays and dramatists, trends and fashions in the theatre, cannot be separate from history. For example, it would be difficult to deny that a play such as Clifford Odets' *Waiting for Lefty* emerged partly from the Depression and the militancy that many on the American Left felt in the face of what they saw as the unfeeling and exploitative attitudes of those who owned big business. It is very much a play of its time, emerging from specific social and historical circumstances. In its chosen 'agit-prop' form and style, the play also reflects an aspect of the contemporary cultural context as well: the idea that theatre had to help change things in society; that playwrights and others in the theatre had a social responsibility to attack injustices and to offer a criticism of established order; and that drama could be used to activate audiences to direct action.

Again, be specific when you make references to historical, social and cultural contexts rather than being vague and general. For example, if a play reflects the widespread feeling of paranoia in 1950s America, be specific in mentioning the causes of such feelings, for example the McCarthyite hearings, the 'Red Scares', the spy scandals. If you are trying to place a particular play within a recognised dramatic form, then, again, be specific: *Winterset* is an example of social drama, notwithstanding its use of dramatic verse. Remember that many plays fit into a generic pattern: that is, they belong to a familiar type of play, a genre with its own conventions, style, subject matter, settings and type of dramatic language. You may want to comment on how a particular play obeys the rules of the genre to which it belongs, and how much it breaks those rules.

Using quotations and textual references

Quotations from the texts of plays are essential to back up thematic analysis or suggestions about how a scene or dialogue should be interpreted. However, use quotations sparingly. It is better to 'pepper' your writing with brief but relevant quotations than to quote long chunks of text. Consider this analysis of the role of Willy Loman in Miller's *Death of a Salesman*:

> In the character of Willy Loman, Miller represents the average American's need to be accepted and to be popular: he has Loman talk about how he is going to be 'bigger than Uncle Charley' in business terms 'because Charley is not liked'. Loman emphasises to his sons Biff and Happy the importance of looking right and making the

correct impression on prospective employers: 'A business suit, and talk as little as possible, and don't crack any jokes.'

It is important to use quotations from the text to illustrate a point you are making, but you may also make close textual references that do not involve actual quotation. Consider this example on the same Miller play:

Miller stresses Biff's sense of frustration and alienation, which is increased by his father's frequent allusions to his son's past glories as a college football star and by the knowledge that his father has 'feet of clay', arising out of the scene when he discovers Willy in a hotel bedroom with a woman.

These references are concrete and specific and illustrate the point that is being made about the character. As a rule, always illustrate a major piece of analysis by quoting from, or referring specifically to, relevant sections of the play text. Try to integrate the quotations from the plays with your analysis of them, so that they become an integral part of your analysis rather than something that is just tagged on for the purposes of illustration.

Interpreting plays and using critical sources

You should read what particular dramatists have written about their plays and what they intended them to be about, but you need not accept dramatists' interpretations of their own work as being the only true 'meaning'. Dramatists may think what they have written means this or that; in fact, to an audience or readers, their plays might mean something quite different. The intentions of the dramatist may, then, be of limited interest. All written texts, plays included, are open to multi-layered interpretation. No two individuals will have exactly the same interpretation of a text because our reading of any text, or our response to a performance, will vary according to numerous factors such as gender and age differences, social class, our own knowledge and experience of the subject matter, personal taste and preferences. Plays in performance are particularly open to varying interpretations because one director and group of actors can produce a very different interpretation and performance of a play text from another director and team of performers. Equally, historical perspective alters our reading of plays: an audience in the 1920s would certainly have seen a play such as O'Neill's *The Hairy Ape* in different terms from an audience viewing it today. Therefore, try to interpret the plays you study from a personal point of view, but make clear what approach you are taking in writing about them. Consider this criticism:

I find Mamet's plays generally excluding because it is such a male world he portrays. Even when female characters are represented, they are invariably victims or *femmes fatales* or variations on that female stereotype. For example, in …

Clearly, this approach is from a gender-centred point of view and as such is a valid criticism.

By all means, refer to critical sources and quote from particular critics when you think it is relevant, but do not overdo this. It is best to use critics to stimulate your own thinking. What most people will be interested in reading is your response to the plays you study and not the opinions of professional critics. However, when critical opinion is used aptly and briefly, then it can help. Consider this:

John Gassner refers to Miller's 'moral passion and taut play writing to the theme of human responsibility' and I think this is an accurate summation of Miller's drama. There is moral passion in *Death of a Salesman* and *The Crucible,* and the need for a sense of social responsibility pervades such plays as *All My Sons* and *A View from the Bridge*.

The critical comment is related to specific plays of the dramatist and thus it illuminates the plays and strengthens the student's argument.

Assignments

1   Divide into groups of four to six. Choose one of the play extracts from Part 3 (pages 59–97). You are going to act out this extract, so one person must take on the role of director. Divide the roles among the rest of the group. Rehearse the acting of the extract, discussing what you, as a group, would want to communicate to an audience in this scene.

   After this exercise has been completed, each of you should write up a detailed account of the rehearsal and performance of the extract, saying how this activity enhanced your understanding of the scene.

2   Read the extracts from *Death of a Salesman* (pages 78–80) and *The American Dream* (pages 88–90). Both these extracts deal with the idea of the American Dream. Contrast how this theme is handled in the two extracts.

3   Say which American play that you have read features the most interesting female character. Discuss why you find this character intriguing and what kind of representation the playwright has created. Use any of the play extracts from Part 3 (pages 59–97) to back up your analysis.

4   Sam Shepard and David Mamet are often described as very 'male-oriented' writers. Basing your analysis on one or two plays by either or both of these writers, discuss the image of masculinity that is represented.

5   Choose one American play from the 1930s and one from the 1950s that seem to you to represent their decade in terms of what was happening in American society at the time. In what ways are the plays representative?

6   Choose one American play, or one extract from Part 3, that you consider to be optimistic about American society *and* one play or extract that takes a rather more pessimistic view. Contrast the picture of America that is represented in dramatic terms by the two plays or extracts.

7   From the American plays you have read, decide which character you would most like to play on stage or in a film version of the relevant play. Write about how you would approach the part and what aspects of the character you would need to represent.

8   If you were a director, which American play would you like to direct and why? Discuss what themes you would want to bring out in a performance of the play and what instructions you would give your cast.

9   Write about one American play that you consider to be interesting for its use of 'theatrical language' and expressiveness, as well as for its themes and what it reflects of American society.

10 Choose one American play that has been adapted for the screen. Discuss how the play was adapted for this different medium and whether you think the play gained or lost from the adaptation.

11 One critic, Alan Trachtenberg, has asked this question about the role of American writers in American society: 'What place for the serious artist in a society without active standards of decency, decorum and moral

intelligence?' Choose one American dramatist and analyse how his or her plays reflect a sense of alienation from American society.

12 American society at different periods of its history has been accused of encouraging conformity and regimentation. Which play or plays seems to represent most vividly these social tendencies?

13 Modernism in the arts seems to stress the need for individuals to escape 'the deadly restraints of monotonous lives or oppressive institutions' (Warren French). In your judgement, which American play or plays represents this need most powerfully? Give your reasons for your opinion, making close references to the text of the play(s).

14 'Playwrights should be creating theatre not sociology.' (John Gassner) Argue the case for or against this statement with reference to at least two American plays of the 20th century.

15 Choose one American playwright and learn as much as you can about his or her life by reading biographies, autobiographies and anything written about, or by, the individual concerned. Then show how far and how effectively, in your opinion, the dramatist has used his or her life experience in the plays he or she has written.

6 | Reading list and other resources

Play texts

The following are invaluable anthologies of American plays with relevant introductions and background detail:

25 Best Plays edited by John Gassner (Crown Publishers, New York, originally published 1949). Includes *The Hairy Ape, Desire under the Elms, The Front Page, What Price Glory?, Street Scene, Gods of the Lightning*

16 Famous American Plays: edited by Cerf and Cartmell (Garden City, originally published in 1941). Contains *The Front Page, The Green Pastures, Ah, Wilderness!, Waiting for Lefty, The Women, Our Town, The Little Foxes* and *The Time of Your Life*

20 Best Plays of the American Theatre edited by John Gassner (Crown Publishers, New York). Contains *Golden Boy, Winterset, High Tor, The Children's Hour*

Best American Plays 1918–1958 edited by Gassner (Crown Publishers, New York). Contains *The Adding Machine, Awake and Sing!* and *Green Grow the Lilacs* by Lynn Riggs, the play on which was based the musical *Oklahoma!*

Best American Plays, third series 1945–1951 edited by John Gassner (Crown Publishers, New York) Contains *Death of a Salesman, A Streetcar Named Desire, The Member of the Wedding, The Iceman Cometh, All My Sons, Come Back, Little Sheba, Anne of the Thousand Days* and *Summer and Smoke*

Best American Plays, seventh series 1967–1973 edited by Clive Barnes (Crown Publishers, New York). Contains *The Price, Indians* and *All Over*

Selected play texts

Eugene O'Neill *Anna Christie/The Emperor Jones; Ah, Wilderness!; Desire under the Elms/The Great God Brown; Mourning Becomes Electra; Strange Interlude; Long Day's Journey into Night*
(All these are published by the National Theatre, London)

Clifford Odets *Golden Boy* (Penguin, Harmondsworth, 1963)

Arthur Miller

Collected Plays (Faber and Faber, 1958) Contains all of Miller's plays up to the mid-1950s and has an invaluable preface by Miller himself

Plays Two (Methuen,1989) Includes *The Misfits, After the Fall, Incident at Vichy, The Price*

Plays Three (Methuen, 1990) Includes *The American Clock, The Archbishop's Ceiling*

All My Sons (Heinemann,1989)

Death of a Salesman (Penguin, 1971)

The Crucible (Penguin, 1972)

Tennessee Williams

A Streetcar Named Desire and Other Plays (Penguin, 1976)

Includes *The Glass Menagerie and Sweet Bird of Youth*

The Rose Tattoo and Other Plays (Penguin, 1977)) Includes *Camino Real* and *Orpheus Descending*

Edward Albee

The American Dream (French, 1960)

David Mamet

American Buffalo (Methuen, 1985)

Oleanna (Dramatists Play Services Ltd., 1995)

Sam Shepard *Seven Plays* (Faber and Faber, 1981)

Introduction by Richard Gilman. Includes *True West, Buried Child, Curse of the Starving Class, The Tooth Crime*

Critical works on American drama: general

C W E Bigsby *A Critical Introduction to Twentieth-Century American Drama* (Cambridge University Press, 1985)

C W E Bigsby *Modern American Drama 1945–1990* (Cambridge University Press, 1992)

G Bordman *The Oxford Companion to the American Theatre* (Oxford University Press, 1984)

B F Dukore *American Dramatists 1918–1945* (Macmillan, 1984)

Boris Ford (ed.) *The New Pelican Guide to English literature: Volume 9: American Literature* (Penguin,1991)

American political, social and cultural history

I Campbell *The USA 1917–1941* (Cambridge University Press, 1998)

P A Carter *Another Part of the Fifties* (Columbia University Press, 1983)

M Dubofsky, A Theokaris and D Smith *The United States in the Twentieth Century* (Prentice Hall, 1978)

G Hodgson *America in Our Time* (Vantage Books, 1978)

D Miller and M Nowak *The Fifties: The Way We Really Were* (Doubleday, 1977)

Film versions of American plays

Below is a list of film versions of many of the plays discussed in this book. Some of these are shown on television from time to time, others are available on video, and the less well-known, older films are sometimes shown in programmes at film theatres dedicated to preserving and exhibiting the art of film. Very often filmed versions of plays necessarily differ from the original plays.

Eugene O'Neill
Anna Christie (1930); *The Emperor Jones* (1933); *Ah, Wilderness!* (1935); *Long Day's Journey into Night* (1961); *The Iceman Cometh* (1973)

Elmer Rice
Street Scene (1931); The Adding Machine (1968)

Ben Hecht and Charles MacArthur
His Girl Friday (1940; version of *The Front Page*); *The Front Page* (1974)

Clifford Odets
Golden Boy (1939); *The Country Girl* (1954); *The Big Knife* (1955)

Maxwell Anderson
Winterset (1936); *Key Largo* (1948)

Robert Sherwood
The Petrified Forest (1936

Lillian Hellman
The Little Foxes (1939); *Watch on the Rhine* (1943)

Thornton Wilder
Our Town (1940)

William Saroyan
The Time of Your Life (1948)

Arthur Miller
All My Sons (1948); *Death of a Salesman* (1951); *The Misfits* (1961); *A View from a Bridge* (1962); *Death of a Salesman* (1985); *The Crucible* (1997)

Tennessee Williams
The Glass Menagerie (1950); *A Streetcar Named Desire* (1951); *Cat on a Hot Tin Roof* (1958); *The Fugitive Kind* (1959); *Suddenly Last Summer* (1959); *Sweet Bird of Youth* (1962)

Carson McCullers
The Member of the Wedding (1953)

Lorraine Hansberry
A Raisin' in the Sun (1961)

William Inge
Come Back Little Sheba (1952); *Picnic* (1955); *The Dark at the Top of the Stairs* (1960)

Edward Albee
Who's Afraid of Virginia Woolf? (1964)

Arthur Kopit
Buffalo Bill and the Indians (1976)

David Mamet
House of Games (1988); *Homicide* (1991); *Glengarry Glen Ross* (1992); *American Buffalo* (1994)

Sam Shepard
Paris Texas (1984); *Fool For Love* (1986)

Glossary of critical terms

Absurdism, or the theatre of the absurd a term used first in the 1960s to describe a type of drama that emphasised the meaninglessness of existence in plays that dispensed with coherent action, 'characters', familiar settings and psychological realism

Agit-prop short for agitation and propaganda: drama that aims to involve audiences with political issues and to persuade them to action

Alienation effect associated with the German playwright Bertolt Brecht, this dramatic technique aims constantly to remind audiences that they are watching a performance, so they can remain emotionally detached from the action and characters of a play

Broadway the term used to describe mainstream American theatre; Broadway is where many of the large, commercial theatres are located in New York. Increasingly, 'serious' American drama has had to be produced off-Broadway or in other American cities

Commercial theatre a term used to describe theatrical performances produced by management companies intent on profit

Dialogue a term used to describe the words characters in a play exchange with one another

Director the individual who has overall artistic responsibility for creating a performance of a dramatic work

Directors' theatre a term used to describe drama that is dominated by a director's concept or vision, as opposed to the dramatist's

Exposition dialogue that explains certain essential facts to the audience about the dramatic situation, the setting and the characters

Expressionism a reaction against realism, expressionism in drama employs expressionist and 'theatrical' devices of sets, design, props, music, gesture, mime, language, costume and sound to create a poetic and 'expressionist' representation of reality

Genre many plays belong to certain familiar types of drama e.g. thrillers, farces, tragedies, musicals. These 'genres' have their conventional themes, settings, characters and plots and usually arouse strong audience expectations

Historical perspective viewing a play (or any work of art) in its historical context and from the perspective of a later era

Intentionalist fallacy   the mistaken idea (fallacy) that a text only means what its author 'intended' it to mean

Melodrama   an intense type of drama that is 'larger-than-life' and aims to provoke strong emotional reactions from an audience through dramatic climaxes, strongly-defined and familiar characters and dramatic situations

Method, The   a technique of acting based on the teachings of the Russian actor and director, Stanislavsky. The Method encourages actors to 'get inside' the character they are playing and use their personal experience to find the emotional centre of a role

Modernism   the movement in the arts that began in Europe in the latter part of the 19th century. Modernism challenged traditional views in the arts by breaking away from conventional forms. It inevitably portrayed the artist as alienated from contemporary society. It more often that not seemed to advocate escape from conformity and regimentation in society and in doing so, modernism's view of 'reality' frequently seemed fragmented, a reflection of the fragmented society the artists were experiencing

Motivation   characters are said to have 'motivations' for their actions. Actors, when preparing to play a part, try to define why their character behaves as s/he does

Naturalism   a more extreme form of realism, naturalism aimed to put a 'slice-of-life' onto the stage by creating the illusion of verisimilitude to everyday reality

Props   stage properties other than costumes, scenery or furniture. Props can 'dress' a set and communicate meaning to an audience, or they can be objects used in the course of the dramatic action (e.g. a gun, a letter, a telegram)

Psychological realism   playwrights may explain the actions of their characters by providing clues to their 'psychology' and motivation. In this way, audiences are encouraged to think of characters as real human beings rather than figures within a dramatic construct

Realism   realism in drama aims to represent on stage everyday reality and the familiar concerns of 'ordinary' people within a recognisable setting. Usually 'realistic' plays end with some clear-cut resolution to the dramatic situation

Set or the setting   the surroundings in which the action of a play is supposed to take place. The set designer is responsible for creating the 'scenery' for a play, which can be very elaborate or simple enough merely to suggest imaginatively a particular setting

Social drama   a kind of 'problem play' that deals dramatically with a social issue by creating characters that symbolise opposing points of view and a plot that represents the issue at work in society

Stage management   the process by which technically a play is staged within a performing space. The **stage manager** may be responsible for a team co-ordinating many aspects of performance: lighting, sound, props, sets, furniture, etc.

Subsidised theatre   theatre that is financially subsidised by government or local authority money to promote the art of theatre. Commercial theatre, by contrast, (e.g. Broadway in New York) survives on the basis of box-office returns

Sub-text   the layer of meaning below the words that are spoken by characters in a play: often a scene is about what is not verbalised by the dramatic figures. Actors and a director often work out a scene from the point of view of its sub-text: what is really being communicated here?

Tragedy   a play that represents the downfall or death of its main dramatic figure(s) through a combination, usually, of circumstances, fate and character flaws. *Death of a Salesman* for example, has been described as a tragedy of an ordinary man; Blanche Dubois in Williams' *A Streetcar Named Desire* could be described as a tragic character

Chronology

Date	Historical/Social	Cultural	American drama
Before 1900	Mass immigration from Europe	Modernism in European theatre and arts; realism still dominates American arts	Realism/lavish spectacle on American stages
1900–15	Immigration peaks; industrialisation and growth of American cities; increasing ethos of materialism	Impact of modernism on American arts: novelists Henry James, Theodore Dreiser, Jack London, Edith Wharton; growing popularity of movies as mass entertainment	1915: Provincetown Players founded to encourage American dramatists
1917–18	American isolationists defeated when US enters WW1; armistice signed 1918		
1919–29	Economic boom: assembly line production, massive increase in car ownership; Jazz Age; Prohibition; organised crime; mistrust of trade unions, 'Red scare' hysteria; black Americans and recent immigrants amongst poorest citizens; women win right to vote	Modernist novelists: Sinclair Lewis, Scott Fitzgerald, Ernest Hemingway; lost generation writers; poetry: T. S. Eliot's 'The Waste Land'; silent movie era ends with invention of soundtracks; importance of radio as mass medium; visual arts: Surrealism, Dadaism, Cubism	O'Neill's modernist plays The Emperor Jones, The Hairy Ape, All God's Chillun; Rice The Adding Machine, Street Scene; Hecht/MacArthur The Front Page; first production of musical Oklahoma
1929	Wall Street crash: world-wide economic crisis ensues		
1929–41	The Great Depression: mass unemployment, banks collapse, farming crisis, millions of Americans living in poverty; Roosevelt's New Deal: social reform, government intervention and investment	American artists' increasing alienation; criticism of failing system and erosion of American ideals; novelists: William Faulkner, John Steinbeck, James T. Farrell, Richard Wright, Thomas Wolfe, Nathaniel West, Eudora Welty; movies: Orson Welles' Citizen Kane	O'Neill Mourning Becomes Electra; Anderson Winterset; Odets Waiting for Lefty, Awake and Sing!, Golden Boy; Hellman The Little Foxes; Wilder Our Town; Saroyan The Time of Your Life
1941	Japanese attack Pearl Harbor, December 1941. America enters WW2		

America at war

1941–45			
1945–60	Atomic bombs dropped on Hiroshima and Nagasaki, 1945; WW2 ends; Cold War starts; 'Red scares' again as Soviet Union explodes atomic bomb, spy scares; Congress investigates communist subversion in government and the arts: McCarthyism and Un-Americanism; Korean War 1950–53; Eisenhower Presidency; unprecedented wealth; flight from cities to suburbs; black Americans struggle for civil rights; women's movement	Novelists: Norman Mailer, Saul Bellow, Mary McCarthy; James Baldwin; beat generation writers: Jack Kerouac, Allen Ginsberg; movies: film noir and epics; dominance of television as mass medium; rock 'n' roll; teen culture	O'Neill *The Iceman Cometh*, *Long Day's Journey into Night*; Williams *The Glass Menagerie*, *A Streetcar Named Desire*, *Cat on a Hot Tin Roof*; Miller *All My Sons*, *Death of a Salesman*, *The Crucible* ; McCullers *The Member of the Wedding*
1960–75	Kennedy elected: 'New Frontier' ideal; Cuban Crisis 1962; civil rights marches; Kennedy assassinated Nov. 1963; President Johnson's 'Great Society'; advances in civil rights for black Americans; US's increasing involvement in Vietnam; peace movement and anti-war demos; assassinations of Martin Luther King and Malcolm X; riots in cities; Nixon elected 1968, 1972; defeat in Vietnam; Watergate – Nixon resigns	Pop art; experimentation: 'happenings'; notion of divide between 'high art' and 'popular art' in question; post modernism; self-conscious ironic fables and magic realism; Hollywood movies chase youthful audiences; new frankness in theatre and cinema	Albee *Zoo Story*, *The American Dream*, *Who's Afraid of Virginia Woolf?*; Miller *After the Fall*, *The Price*; Baldwin *Blues for Mister Charlie*; Kopit *Indians*
1975–90	Presidents Bush and Carter trying to heal divisions in society; growing fragmentation of American society; concern about drug use and rise in crime; 1980 Reagan elected: conservative agenda, appeal to patriotism, 'greed is good' ethic; collapse of communism in Eastern Europe; end of Cold War	Minimalism in arts; debates over political correctness; Hollywood movies dominated by computer technology and special effects; dominance of pop culture; 'high culture' under threat?	Sam Shepard and David Mamet; Broadway dominated by musicals

Index

Acknowledgements

The author and publishers wish to thank the following for permission to use copyright material:

The James Baldwin Estate for an extract from James Baldwin *Blues for Mister Charlie*, pp. 46–49. Copyright ©1964 by James Baldwin, copyright renewed; Bantam Books, a division of Random House, Inc, for an extract from Sam Shepard 'Buried Child' from *Seven Plays by Sam Shepard*, pp. 91–93. Copyright ©1979 by Sam Shepard; Casarotto Ramsey & Associates Ltd on behalf of The University of the South, Sewanee, Tennessee and New Directions Publishing Corporation for an extract from Tennessee Williams *A Streetcar Named Desire*. Copyright ©1947 by Tennessee Williams; Robert A Freedman Dramatic Agency, Inc for an extract from Maxwell Anderson *Winterset*, pp. 6–7. Copyright ©1935 under title *Wintersong* by Quentin Anderson and Maxwell Anderson. Copyright renewal ©1963 by Gilda Anderson, Alan Anderson, Terence Anderson, Quentin Anderson and Hesper Anderson. Copyright ©1946 under title *Winterset* by Maxwell Anderson. Copyright renewal ©1973 by Gilda Anderson, Alan Anderson, Terence Anderson, Quentin Anderson and Hesper Anderson; Samuel French, Inc for an extract from Elmer Rice *The Adding Machine*, pp. 101–102. Copyright ©1922, 1929 by Elmer Rice. Copyright ©1923 by Doubleday, Page & Co. Copyright ©1949 (in renewal) by Elmer Rice. Copyright ©1950 (in renewal) by Elmer Rice. Copyright ©1956 (in renewal) by Elmer Rice; Methuen Publishing Ltd for an extract from Arthur Kopit *Indians* (1968) pp. 305–306; William Morrow Agency for an extract from Ben Hecht and Charles MacArthur *The Front Page* (1928) p. 481. Copyright ©1928 by Cayben Productions and Charles MacArthur. Copyright © 1928 by Ben Hecht and Charles MacArthur. Copyright ©1950 (Acting Edition) by Ben Hecht and Charles MacArthur. Copyright ©1955 (in renewal) by Ben Hecht and Charles MacArthur; Laurence Pollinger Ltd on behalf of the Estate of the Author for an extract from Carson McCullers *A Member of the Wedding*, pp. 190–191; Random House UK for an extract from Edward Albee 'The American Dream' from *Zoo Story and Other Plays* (1961), Jonathan Cape, pp. 50–51; and with Random House, Inc for extracts from Eugene O'Neill *The Iceman Cometh*, Jonathan Cape, pp. 104–105. Copyright ©1946 by Eugene O'Neill; and Eugene O'Neill *The Hairy Ape*, Jonathan Cape, pp. 20–21. Copyright ©1922 and renewed 1950 by Eugene O'Neill; Random House, Inc for an extract from Lillian Hellman *The Little Foxes*. Copyright ©1930 and renewed 1967 by Lillian Hellman; Rogers, Coleridge & White Ltd in association with International Creative Management on behalf of the author for extracts from Arthur Miller *The Crucible*, pp. 47–50. Copyright ©1952, 1953, 1954 by Arthur Miller, renewed 1980, 1981, 1982; and Arthur Miller *Death of a Salesman*, pp. 27–28. Copyright ©1948, 1949, 1951 by Arthur Miller, renewed 1975, 1976, 1980.

Every effort has been made to reach copyright holders; the publishers would like to hear from anyone whose rights they have unknowingly infringed.